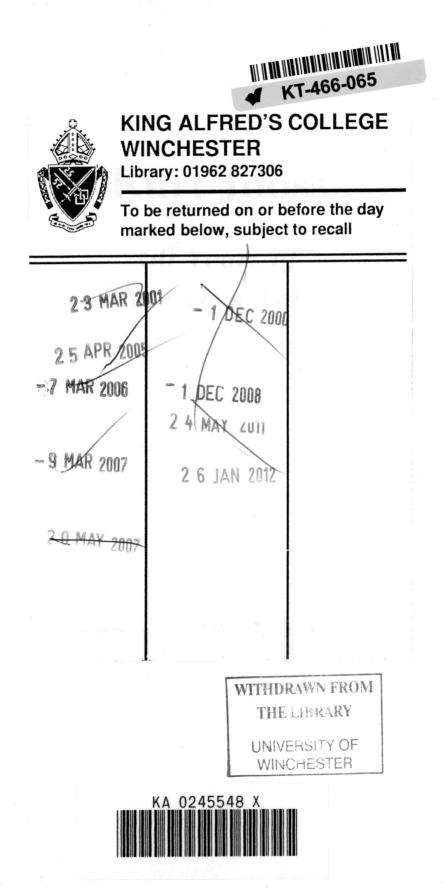

Kurt Jooss

60 Years of
The Green Table

Proceedings of the conference held at
The University of Birmingham
17-19 October 1992

Edited by

Andy Adamson   Clare Lidbury

The University of Birmingham

Studies in Drama and Dance

©   1994   The University of Birmingham

First published 1994

Adamson, Andy and Lidbury, Clare
     Kurt Jooss: 60 years of *The Green Table.*
     (Studies in Drama and Dance)

     ISBN 0-7044-1418X

Cover photo: Joseph Cipollo as Death by Leslie E. Spatt

Designed and typeset by Andy Adamson
at the Department of Drama and Theatre Arts
The University of Birmingham

Published by
The University of Birmingham
Edgbaston Birmingham B15 2TT

Contents

Acknowledgements

The conference could not have taken place without close collaboration between The Birmingham Royal Ballet and The University of Birmingham. We are extremely grateful to Sir Peter Wright, Director of The Birmingham Royal Ballet and Professor Michael Robinson, Head of The Department of Drama and Theatre Arts, for making this possible. The conference programme was devised by Andy Adamson and Jill Henderson, former Education Officer of The Birmingham Royal Ballet. Alison Maconochie was the conference administrator assisted by Clare Lidbury.

We are grateful to have received financial assistance from Birmingham City Council and British Airways PLC., while the editing of these papers presented at the conference was made possible by a grant from the Sir Barry Jackson Trust.

We would also like to thank: Craig Burman; Jim Fraser; Jim Hanrahan; Magdelene Hardy; Anna Markard; Hermann Markard; press and marketing staff of The Birmingham Royal Ballet; Sandy Robertson; Ross Williams.

Notes on Contributors

Valerie Preston-Dunlop is head of sponsored research at the Laban Centre for Movement and Dance and Director of the Laban Collection project. A student of Laban's for 12 years, she now heads the Choreological Studies Faculty at the Laban Centre, which is pioneering the development of Laban's work for the 1990s. She has an international reputation as a teacher and expert on Laban's work.

Clare Lidbury studied with Andy Adamson and Jane Winearls and now lectures at The University of Birmingham. Her doctoral research focussed on the work of Kurt Jooss and specifically on *The Green Table*. She is a choreographer and teacher exploring the theories developed by Kurt Jooss and Sigurd Leeder.

Andy Adamson studied at The University of Birmingham with Jane Winearls. He is now Lecturer in Dance in the Department of Drama and Theatre Arts where he has introduced a new undergraduate degree programme in Dance and Theatre Arts. Andy Adamson is also responsible for developing CALABAN - a computer aided Labanotation programme for producing specialist Labanotation scores and for computer based analysis. He is both a choreographer and a teacher with specific interest in the development of the integrated performer where inner understanding is as important as outer technique.

Peter Wright studied with Kurt Jooss, Vera Volkova and Peggy van Praagh. He danced with the Ballets Jooss after World War ll and also with the Sadler's Wells Theatre Ballet. His career moved swiftly from dancer to that of teacher/choreographer/interpreter and he became balletmaster for the Stuttgart Ballet (1961-67), under the directorship of John Cranko. In 1970 he became Associate Director of the Royal Ballet and was appointed as Resident Director of the Royal Ballet Touring Company in 1975, the company which subsequently became Sadler's Wells Royal Ballet and most recently The Birmingham Royal Ballet.

Anna Markard was born in Essen, Germany and grew up in England. She began her training with Sigurd Leeder and returned to Germany to continue her studies at the Folkwangschule, Essen, under her father Kurt Jooss. She also studied classical ballet with Nora Kiss in Paris. Her professional career began in 1954 as a member of the Ballet Company of the Düsseldorf Opera House and she also began to teach, first in Germany, later becoming a member of the Dance Faculty of Butler University, Indianapolis, USA. She was subsequently closely associated with the Folkwang Hochschule and helped coach the newly formed Folkwang Ballet as well as acting as director on the company's extensive European tours. Working in close collaboration with her father, she has reconstructed several of his earlier works. Her staging of Jooss's repertoire has associated her with companies all over the world.

Hermann Markard studied painting at several art academies in Germany and the USA. His debut as a stage designer was for the Opera Theatre of the Julliard School of Music in New York in 1960. He became lighting designer for the Essen Folkwang Ballet and Het National Ballet in Amsterdam. He designs sets, costumes and lighting for opera and ballet working with Jooss (*Afternoon of a Faun*, 1965, and *Phases*, 1966, for the Folkwang Ballet), Jean Cébron and Pina Bausch. Other activities include directing and designing for opera and television, teaching stage design and exhibiting his own work.

Mikaela Polley began dancing at the age of three and went on to study with Elsbeth Nunn as well as attending Saturday classes at the Central School of Ballet. She joined the Royal Ballet Upper School in 1988 and Tbe Birmingham Royal Ballet Company in 1990. Since then she has danced small roles in *The Sleeping Beauty* and *Romeo and Juliet*, a principal part in Paul Taylor's *Airs* and the role of the Young Girl in *The Green Table*.

Introduction

Dance has existed at The University of Birmingham since 1965 when the first lecturer in dance at a British University was appointed to the Department of Physical Education. She was Jane Winearls, a dancer and choreographer, pupil of Sigurd Leeder, teacher for Kurt Jooss at the Folkwangschule in Essen and friend of Rudolf Laban. In 1978, with the appointment of Andy Adamson and the creation of a degree in Music, Drama and Dance (BA Hons.), the lectureship was moved to the Department of Drama and Theatre Arts. Since then dance has flourished. At undergraduate level a new degree course in Dance and Theatre Arts has been established, while at postgraduate level, a taught MA course is offered, together with research degrees leading to M.Phil. and PhD.

The basis of dance teaching in the department continues to be that initiated by Jane Winearls - a method based on the work of Laban, Jooss and Leeder. This approach enables the dance practitioner to consider his/her art also from an intellectual standpoint. It provides a 'language of dance' for use in both practical and academic contexts and, combined with the Labanotation system of movement documentation and analysis, it makes an ideal system for dance education within a university context. This is particularly the case within a university department which has pioneered a course centred on the work of the performer, and whose ethos is the integration of academic and practical study.

It is against this background that the programme for the Jooss Conference was devised, with the aim that practical dance classes should inform the analytical and critical papers presented at the conference. Anna Markard was engaged to teach a repertoire class, based on extracts from *The Green Table*, and, in the original programme, Jean Cébron from the Folkwangschule would have contributed improvisation and dance technique classes in the Jooss-Leeder style. Unfortunately M.Cébron was forced to withdraw at the last moment, and these classes were given by Andy Adamson and Clare Lidbury.

Prior to the presentation of papers conference delegates viewed a video recording of *The Green Table* by the Joffrey Ballet Company. The first day of papers and classes concluded with an evening dress rehearsal of *The Green Table* given by The Birmingham Royal Ballet at the Birmingham Hippodrome.

A formal link between The Department of Drama and Theatre Arts and The Birmingham Royal Ballet was established in 1991, at the same time as the new degree course in Dance and Theatre Arts. Initially this was through the appointment of Peter Wright as a special Professor in Dance in the School of Performance Studies, but later expanded as dancers and staff of The Birmingham Royal Ballet began providing both practical and academic support for the University course.

Sir Peter Wright's own dance background with the Ballets Jooss was an immediate point of contact between the two institutions and perhaps it was inevitable that at some point the Company would take into its repertoire one of the most important works of the twentieth century, by a choreographer whom Sir Peter acknowledges was a most influential figure in his development. *The Green Table* is widely staged elsewhere in Europe and in the USA but had not been performed in England for many years. Thus with The Birmingham Royal Ballet's staging of *The Green Table* and the Jooss-link between Sir Peter Wright and The University of Birmingham, a conference to celebrate this important occasion was devised.

*   *   *

The Jooss Conference is part of an on-going series of conferences, held at The University of Birmingham, which investigate various aspects of theatre practice.

Le Grand Concours de Chorégraphie, 1932

Dr Clare Lidbury

Kurt Jooss's *The Green Table* celebrated in 1992 the sixtieth anniversary of its premiere at the Paris Choreography Competition of 1932. *Le Grand Concours Internationale de Chorégraphie* was organised by *Les Archives Internationales de la Danse*. This organisation was established in 1931 by Rolf de Maré, a Swedish balletomane and patron of the arts. In 1920, de Maré had created Les Ballets Suèdois for which the choreographer and chief male dancer was Jean Borlin who produced many remarkable works for the company, including *Le Creation du Monde* (1923) and *Relâche* (1924). His untimely death in 1930 led to the founding of *Les Archives Internationales de la Danse* by de Maré in memory of Borlin.

The aims and ideals of the *Archives Internationale de la Danse* (A.I.D.), set out in the preliminary issue of *Les Archives Internationales de la Danse*[1] from October 1932, are many and formidable. One of the aims was the organising of competitions, the first of which being the Choreography Competition of 1932.

The rules of the competition sent out to each contestant and laid down in the preliminary edition of *Les Archives Internationales de la Danse*,[2] stated that the ballets presented should 1) last no less than twelve minutes and be no more than thirty minutes long; 2) that there was to be a minimum of six dancers but no maximum number; 3) that details of the ballets (e.g. title, book, choreographer and designer) were to be submitted in advance and 4) that enrolment had to be made by May 3rd 1932. Further details of organisation listed in the article stated when and where the competition would take place, that the ballets would be presented in front of grey curtains, although additional decor for individual ballets was permitted, and that an orchestra of sixteen musicians would be available. All contestants were to be responsible for their own music and properties with one rehearsal of forty-five minutes with the orchestra, a thirty minute

rehearsal for lighting and a mere fifteen minutes permitted for erect-
ing the scenery. The rules stated that contestants could incur costs of
up to five hundred francs if they withdrew without due notice, that if
there were too many groups wanting to participate the jury would
decide who should compete and that the A.I.D. reserved the right to
film the contestants, with the choreographers retaining the rights to
their ballets but the film being the copyright of the A.I.D. Lastly, the
A.I.D. reserved the right to present the winning ballet in Paris for fifteen days after the competition.

The rules, then, were quite strict regarding the organisational
details of the competition but very free regarding the actual composi-
tions to be presented, for it seems that choreographers were at liberty
to present work in any style or form about anything they chose. As
long as at least six dancers performed for between twelve and thirty
minutes then the criteria would be met. In effect the rules allowed for
any form of dance - classical ballet, modern dance, national, folk and
any combination or synthesis of these or other dance forms, thus
opening the competition to all. Perhaps this reflects the awareness of
the competition organisers of the wide range of dance being explored
at the time.

The competition was intended to be a significant event in the
dance calendar of 1932 - participation was by invitation only and the
prizes, 60,000 Ff. and two weeks of performances at a major Parisian
theatre, were significant in those high-unemployment, financially
problematic times. Although there were some notable absences from
the list of participants (no representation from Britain or from the
United States, and little from the Classical School, for example), the
French press clearly considered the competition as a major event with
coverage appearing in many magazines and journals. With so many
German competitors the German press was also well represented. Dr.
Arthur Michel, a renowned critic and supporter of modern dance in
Germany, wrote in praise of the competition in *Vossiche Zeitung*[3]
stressing its importance for the development of theatrical dance in
Europe. Other critics also praised the A.I.D. and Rolf de Maré in par-
ticular, for organising the competition.

2

There was one negative voice amongst all the praise however, from a great supporter of the classical dance, the influential André Levinson. In *Comoedia*, a journal that had supported the competition from its inception, Levinson wrote that the rules had not given any chance to classical choreography.[4] Rolf de Maré's reply, also in *Comoedia*, to the accusation that in effect German modern dance had been favoured at the expense of French classical dance insisted that the competition had been open to all, including the classical companies of Russia and France, as well as the modern German, Polish and Austrian groups.[5] The rest of the press evidently were not against German modern dance, but several agreed with Levinson's regret at the lack of representation from France.

In the light of Levinson's criticism it is interesting to consider the personnel responsible for judging the competition. Details of the jury were laid down in the *Réglements des Concours* under articles 17-19.[6] These state that the jury would be designated by the Archives Internationales de la Danse; that it would be composed of two choreographers from different schools, a dancer, a conductor, two theatre directors, a designer, a painter, a film maker, 'un homme de lettres' and one of the committee of the A.I.D. The *Réglements* also give details of the criteria for the assessment of each of the dance pieces competing. The jury would take into consideration the group as a whole, individual (solo) dances, the costumes, the music and the work in its entirety. Article 19 notes that the jury had the right to modify the sharing of the prizes, and not to award prizes at all if it judged the presentations to be sub-standard. In the event the composition of the jury was somewhat different. Who these people were, their backgrounds in dance and the other arts are important considerations in assessing the credibility and standing of the winners of the competition.

The A.I.D. was represented by Rolf de Maré. His background with the avant-garde *Les Ballets Suédois* and as a patron of the arts ensured that he brought a breadth of knowledge to the jury. The two choreographers were both from the school of modern dance - Rudolf

Laban and Max Terpis. At the time of the competition Laban was ballet director at the Berlin Staatsoper. He brought to the jury his wealth of experience as a dancer, choreographer, teacher and theorist in Modern Dance. Max Terpis was a dancer and choreographer as well as a teacher. At the 1927 Dance Congress he stated his admiration for both Wigman and Pavlova, maintaining that the difference between classical ballet and modern dance was merely a difference between categories and approaches and not a difference in quality, suggesting that Terpis would have viewed the competitors from both schools with equal interest.

Albert Aveline, one of three dancers on the jury, had danced with (and choreographed for) the Paris Opéra Ballet. The other two dancers on the jury also represented the Classical School - Carlotta Zambelli had trained at La Scala, but her career had centred almost exclusively at the Paris Opéra, and after retiring from performing had turned to teaching. Alexandre Volinine had been a *premier danseur* with the Bolshoi Company and was a teacher of some renown, his pupils including David Lichine and Jean Babilée.

Of the musicians, Vladimir Golschmann, had been conductor for Diaghilev's Ballet Russe between 1919 and 1923, then becoming conductor for Les Ballet Suédois. Having worked with two such prestigious forward-thinking ballet companies, Golschmann was in an excellent position to contribute to the jury's deliberations. Florent Schmitt, a composer, was at the time of the competition, music critic for *Le Temps* and as such was an influential figure. Gabriel Astruc was a producer, music publisher and impresario, noted for his receptiveness to new ideas in music, and founder of *La Société Musicale*, a journal for the promotion of new music. He was clearly a far-sighted man with a background in, and knowledge of, music and ballet.

Of the two theatre directors Henri Varna had experience as a revue artist, comedian, and designer. He had also managed several theatres in Paris and at the time of the competition was manager of the *Casino de Paris* (renowned for its spectacular revues), and it was in this theatre that the winning ballets were to be presented after the competition. Prince Serge Volkonsky had been Director of the

Imperial Theatres in Moscow, from 1899-1902, showing considerable sympathy for the advanced ideas of the artists surrounding Diaghilev. Forced to resign from his post, Volkonsky retained his love of ballet, travelling widely and promoting interest in the work of Delsarte and Dalcroze.

With regard to the artists on the jury André Masson had a range of experience as a painter, sculptor, engraver and stage designer. Fernand Léger had designed several ballets for Les Ballet Suédois including *Skating Rink* (1922) and *La Création du Monde* (1923). His experience with Les Ballets Suédois as designer and artist would have given him particular insight into the design/decor elements of the competition.

The so called "L'homme de Lettres" on the jury was Pierre Tugal. Together with Rolf de Maré he co-founded *Les Archives Internationales de la Danse* and later became its curator from 1931-1952. He wrote several articles and books on dance, contributing much to the A.I.D.'s own publications. Tugal may be seen as representing neutral ground on the jury and was a non-voting member.

Thus the members of the jury represented all the arts connected with the presentation of dance in a theatrical context - dancers, choreographers, designers, composers, conductors, theatre directors and impresarios. Of the fourteen jury members, only five were connected directly with dance, of which three were of the classical school (Zambelli, Aveline and Volinine) with Laban and Terpis belonging to the modern school. Of the remaining nine jurists, the musicians and the two designers had connections with classical ballet through their links with the Ballet Suédois. Rolf de Maré had founded that classically based company and Astruc had links with the Ballet Russe. Only Varna and Tugal seemed to have had no allegiance to either school. Overall then, the members of the jury inclined towards the classical school in terms of background and experience, although, of course, Les Ballets Suédois and the Ballet Russe were avant-garde classical companies, with their choreographers exploring and devising dance vocabularies outside of the academic, classical school.

It is interesting that in this *Concours de Chorégraphie*, apparently the first choreography competition of its kind, only two jury members were experienced choreographers and both of those from the modern school. However, a letter dated 22nd January 1932 from Tugal to Jooss, suggests that another choreographer of great renown was intended to be on the jury:

> "Die Jury - Richter für choreographie sind: Michel
> Fokine und Herr von Laban"

This states clearly that both Fokine and Laban were to be judges. The presence of Fokine - an experienced classical choreographer with pronounced views on what ballet (and dance) should be - may have given rather a different slant to the composition of the jury. However, it would seem that Fokine either turned down his invitation to partici-pate or withdrew from the jury, his place being taken by Max Terpis - well known inside Germany as a choreographer from the modern school, but with nothing like Fokine's international reputation.

The only other jury member with active choreographic experience was Aveline. Doubtless the other dancers (Zambelli and Volinine) would most likely have experienced being choreographed on, and the musicians and designers may have been involved in watching the process of choreography. Nonetheless, the composition of the jury reflects the various elements of the dance works which were to be assessed - the choreography of solo and group dances, the costumes, music, and the complete effect of the whole. The jury presented, then, a varied and interesting panel, bringing to the competition a range of backgrounds and experience only matched by that of the variety of the competitors themselves.

The competition was held over the three evenings of July 2nd, 3rd, and 4th, 1932, commencing at 8pm. Six or seven ballets were presented each evening, and as each ballet could be up to half an hour in length, the evenings must have been somewhat of an endurance test. The range in style of the ballets represented the wide variety in background, training and experience of the competitors. However, the programme for each of the three evenings appears to have been carefully planned with each night seeing a range of works in terms of style, theme and accompaniment. Details of the individual pieces are given in the programme for the competition while an article, *"Les Participants au Concours de Chorégraphie, 1932"* published in the first edition of *Les Archives Internationales de la Danse*, outlines the working methods of the choreographers. It seems likely that these were submitted by the choreographers themselves prior to the competition.

The opening event was a classical ballet choreographed by the French Pierre Conté and performed by his group. He paid particular attention to the decor of his piece, believing that it was extremely important in the way that it enhanced the theme. *La Legende* used music by Debussy, Borodin, Ravel and Monton with designs by Clédon. The second piece, *Contrastes*, was presented by a group from the Dalcroze School - the Austrian La Groupe Hellerau-Laxenburg - with choreography by the director of the group and school, Rosalie Chladek. With music by Handel and Prokofiev, the piece explored the notion that it is rhythm that contributes most to the development of harmonious movement.

Caird Leslie's *Apollon et Daphne* which came next, was based on choreographic forms from the 17th and 18th centuries - the passepied, minuet and courante. These were presented in a stylised form but, while attempting to be true to the music of Rameau, they remained firmly in the tradition of 19th century classical dance. This group was followed by the Polish Irena Prusicka's *Le Sourine de Pulcinelle* with music by Debussy, Schumann and others. She maintained that in her work she was presenting a new idea where the music was in harmony with the choreographic motif.

Boris Kniaseff, a Russian dancer, teacher and choreographer came next with his ballet *La Légende du bouleau*. It presented his idea that dance was an animated poem, both rhythmic and harmonic. The presentation by Le ballet Dorothée Gunther which followed would have been a contrast yet again. *Miniatures* was choreographed by Maja Lex, adhering to the principles of Dorothée Gunther. She believed that there should be a fusion of music and dance, but with

7

the dance created first and the music established after. This group came with its own orchestra - of tambours, timpani, flutes, and gongs - to play music by Gunthild Keetman. The final presentation of that first evening was by the Latvian Anna Kerre. Her piece, *Rêverie*, to music by Chopin, sought to unite the principles of Duncan and Delsarte but also demanded a solid dance technique, precise mime skills, and musical sensitivity.

Kerre's piece must have contrasted greatly with the austerity of the Gunther School's piece, the poetic Kniaseff piece, the expressive work of Prusicka and the historically based ballet of Leslie. The range of musical accompaniment used was as varied as the dance forms, from the percussion orchestra of the Gunther school to Classical Schumann, neo-Classical Prokofiev, Impressionist Debussy and Baroque Rameau. It must, then, have been an extraordinary evening's entertainment with such diverse presentations. Some of the ballets must have been quite interesting, for Chladek, Gunther and Kniaseff were all named as prize winners, suggesting that at least three of the seven presentations on the first evening were of high quality.

The second evening opened with the ballet *La Flamme*, choreographed by the Russian Lubow Egorova and performed by her company. Her piece was dedicated to Anna Pavlova, with whom she had danced in 1907. Egorova believed in the importance of the ensemble (who needed harmony and precision) but for her, faultless technique was the most important thing. The Czech Jarmila Kroschlova's group which followed was of a very different kind. Her *L'Aprés midi d'un jour d'été*, with music by Vaclav Smatacek and costumes by Boska Nerola-Öra, was a narrative ballet for several women, with characters such as birds (geese and peacocks, for example), a cat, and a "l'Oiseau des Rêves".

Next came a national dance item, *Images Polonaises*, presented by the Polish group of Tacyanna Wysocka, described as an ensemble of dances in four tableaux each containing two or three national dances (polka, krakovak, and mazurka, for example). The contrast between the two Polish groups, both from Warsaw, perhaps typifies

8

that of the whole competition. It would be hard for the two groups to be more different with Prusicka's eclectic Wigman-Dalcroze-Ballet background and Wysocka's national dance.

Kurt Jooss's ballet was presented as the fourth item of the second evening. *The Green Table* must have seemed entirely different from the expressive movement, national dance and balletic style of the earlier items. The topicality of Jooss's subject matter, the way in which the ballet was formed by its content, that the ballet was communicating on an intellectual level as well as on an aesthetic level, and that the ballet was actually commentating on real life, cannot but have made a huge impression on the audience and jury alike:

> "Well that [the reception] was incredible. They
> nearly clapped through the whole piece, which was
> dreadful, but of course we liked it because it
> showed us that we had succeeded".[7]

The companies coming after Jooss would clearly have had a hard act to follow. *L'Abandon Celeste* by Janine Solane used music by Wagner. She seems to have been a 'French Isadora' accompanied by a group of children. The final piece of the evening was by the Yugoslavian couple Pia and Pino Mlakar. Their ballet, *Un Amour au moyen age*, with music by Vivaldi, Handel and Bach, was aiming to use the virtuoso technique of classical ballet but with original choreography within the form of theme and variations.

This second evening of competition then was as varied in style and quality as the first night. One can only presume that *The Green Table* was the highlight of the evening with only one other of the ballets from this evening (*Images Polonaises*) being mentioned as a prize winner.

The final evening began with the Swedish Astrid Malmborg's *Rhapsody in Blue*. She took her inspiration from classical ballet, the German school and also from jazz, which she saw as representing the spirit of the age. She was followed by *Les Femmes d'autres cieux*, a *poeme chorégraphique*, presented by Le Ballet d'Ursel Renate Hirt from Berlin, who sought to move outside an imposed technique and rigid rules of choreography. Next came Trudi Schoop's presentation - *Fridolen en Route* - described as a 'pantomime-comique'. She danced the role of Fridolen - "un homme drôle" - herself, displaying her talents as a dancer-comedienne.

Oscar Schlemmer's *Le Ballet Triadique* which came next, must have been one of the more extraordinary events presented at the competition. The costumes, perhaps the most important element of the ballet, sought to eliminate the humanity of the dancer, aiming for abstraction, with the shape of the costume determining the character. Aside from *The Green Table* it seems to be the only other work surviving from the competition. Why Schlemmer's work, created in the early 1920s and performed several times over that decade, should have been accepted is a mystery because Jooss recalled that all the works presented at the competition had to be premieres.[8] For the competition, however, the ballet took a somewhat altered form from the original; for example, the twelve scenes were cut to six and the number of dancers increased from three to seven .

Schlemmer's piece was followed by Gertrude Bodenwieser's *Les Heures solennelles*. It was in two tableaux - *Les Grandes heures* with music by Tcherepine and *Visions de l'époque* to music by Mayer-Lorber - and explored her belief that rhythm was the inspiring force in dance. The final presentation of the third evening and thus of the whole competition was *Le Souffle de printemps*, a ballet divertissement, by the classically trained Russian, Lydia Nesterovskaya. It was a series of solos, duets, trios and group pieces to music by Chopin and Johann Strauss.

These then were the competitors in that first choreographic competition. It is clear that each evening would have had pieces ranging in quality, in a variety of styles, and presentations covering a huge range of themes and subjects. Kurt Jooss's thoughts on his fellow competitors are interesting. He said "a few were very good" and he found Trudi Schoop's piece "very amusing". He thought Chladek's piece was "a very beautiful abstract ballet" but also stated categorically that there were: "some very experimental things... and some were rather rubbish." [9]

It is agreed by all - historians, contemporary critics and writers - that Jooss won the competition though there seems to be confusion over the other prize-winners. Jooss states that Chladek won second prize,[10] while Chujoy and Manchester say it was Schoop [11] and Hall says it was Kniaseff.[12] The winner of the third prize is equally disputed (Mlakar, Gunther or Bodenwieser). It seems likely that the Jury awarded more than the intended one second prize and one third prize. Indeed, in the review *Cahiers d'Art"* Fernand Léger wrote:

> "Six troupes ont gagné la gageur; *Les Contrastes* (Hellerau), *Miniatures* (Gunther), *Images Polonaises* (Prusicka) *La Table Verte* (Jooss), *Fridolen en Route* (Trudi Schoop) *Le Ballet Triadique* (Schlemmer)." [13]

Eduard Szamba, Paris correspondent for *Der Tanz*, [14] would seem to clarify the situation by stating the points which the top ten ballets in the competition were awarded. Out of a possible 1300 points, *The Green Table* scored 1242 points, second placed Chladek scored 1048 and third placed Gunther 1079. In fact this confuses the issue because Gunther's total appears higher than Chladek's (perhaps Chladek's point score should be either 1148 or 1084). This may be one of the reasons why there is such confusion over the other prize winners. The order of the other seven ballets in the top ten was Schoop (985), Kniaseff (972), Schlemmer (780), Kroschlova (772), Bodenwieser (707), Egorova (653) and Mlakar (632). Szamba continues that the ballets by Malmborg and Gregory were also worthy of distinction, but misses out altogether one of Léger's prize winners (Prusicka).

The twenty competitors, representing nine countries, show the diverse state that dance was in at that time. The several schools of modern dance were moving in their own directions, discovering their own dance languages with which to communicate, while choreographers from the classical tradition seem to have been attempting to move onwards by cloaking the classical vocabulary in a variety of ways. From the list of the top ten given by Szamba the majority of choreographers are from the Modern School, with only Kniaseff, Egorova and possibly the Mlakars from the Classical School. These companies, then, actually did rather well because the odds were somewhat against the Classical school with only five of all the participants working in that style. Most of the rest seem to have been either Duncan, Laban or Dalcroze influenced, the exceptions being the more individualistic Schoop and Schlemmer.

A second reason for the classical pieces being less successful may have been that the jury were mainly from the classical school, with the three dancers on the jury being some of the best of their generation. The expectation of the classically influenced jury members of the classical competitors must have been extremely high from a technical as well as choreographic point of view. Thus those modern companies who placed emphasis on areas other than technique may have been at a distinct advantage.

Thirdly, it is known that those prize winners from the modern school had been assimilating and building their ideas for some time, with several of them having schools to train the dancers in their way of thinking and moving before they progressed into the performance groups - Jooss for example had been working on his ideas for a long time and had worked with some of his dancers for seven or eight years. These modern companies were trying to find either a new way of moving or were developing a new vocabulary, in order to present their ideas. Those choreographers working within the academic classical vocabulary may have had difficulty in superimposing their ideas on top of this basic training, rather than allowing their ideas to grow alongside a developing vocabulary. Finally, of course, the majority of the pieces presented may just have been inferior to the winners - either in form, content or in the standard of performance.

The jury and the other people who attended all three nights of the competition witnessed a variety of work, the like of which has probably not been seen before or since. To have drawn together such a range of competitors at such a formative time in the evolution of modern dance was a remarkable achievement. The competition, although receiving much coverage in the French and German press, hardly got a mention in England. Only *The Dancing Times* seems to have carried any coverage of the competition through a brief report by L.Franc Schauer in August 1932 and through Lewitan's "The Month in Germany".[15] He writes about the German groups and the ones which may be considered German - i.e. those works presented by Schoop and Chladek. Of the winner he writes comparatively little, and suggests that Jooss's victory was rather hollow, given the absence of "many great choreographers." He hoped that: "for the sake of the evolution of Dance" the Germans would receive some serious opposition in the next competition.

Exactly how Jooss's work compared with the others is impossible to tell as there seems to be no visual record other than a few photographs of the majority of the other ballets presented. (No trace can be found of the film that was proposed by the A.I.D. in the competition regulations.) In addition several of the choreographers, e.g. Caird Leslie, Anna Kerre and Janine Solane, seem to have disappeared without trace, while others - Kniaseff and Egorova, for example - are remembered for their careers as dancers rather than for their choreographic efforts. On the other hand it is clear that some of the other competitors work was of a very high standard. Schoop particularly went on to tour very successfully in the United States, Chladek continued teaching and choreographing to great acclaim for many years, while Schlemmer's work is well respected and researched. Therefore in spite of what Lewitan says, it would seem that Jooss faced very hard competition for the first prize.

Nonetheless, one may wonder how well Jooss would have fared if any of the Americans (Humphrey or Graham), Russians (Balanchine or Lifar), or English (Ashton or de Valois), had competed. It is, however, very possible that *The Green Table* with its contemporary subject matter, its unique dance language, its simple but effective designs, its original music, its fine dancers and its superb crafting in terms of composition may still have been judged the worthy prize winner. The fact that it has been in the repertoire of companies all over the world must be testament to *The Green Table*'s valid claim to be an honourable winner, paving the way for it to become a classical work of the modern dance repertoire.

Notes

[1] '*Les Archives Internationales de la Danse*' in *Les Archives Internationales de la Danse* (Preliminary Issue, October 1932), pp. 2-3.

[2] *Ibid.* p. 4.

[3] '*Appreciations*', *Les Archives Internationales de la Danse* (No. 1, January 1933), p. 29.

[4] *Ibid.* p. 30.

[5] *Ibid.* p. 29.

[6] '*Réglements de Concours*', *Les Archives Internationales de la Danse* (Preliminary Edition, October 1932), p. 4.

[7] Michael Huxley, '*The Green Table* - A Dance of Death', *Ballett International* (July /August 1982), p. 10.

[8] Kurt Jooss, ' *The Kurt Jooss Lectures*' (Hull University avc. 1972.)

[9] *Ibid.*

[10] *Ibid.*

[11] Anatole Chujoy and P. W. Manchester (Editors) *Encyclopaedia of Ballet and Dance* (New York: Simon and Schuster, 1967), p. 60.

[12] Fernau Hall, *Modern English Ballet* (London: Andrew Melrose, c. 1949), p. 62.

[13] '*Appreciations*', *Les Archives Internationales de la Danse* (No. 1, January 1933), p. 29.

[14] Eduard Szamba, '*Tanzbriefe*', *Der Tanz* (August 1932,) pp. 6-8.

[15] Joseph Lewitan, 'The Month in Germany', *The Dancing Times* (September 1932), p. 465.

Kurt Jooss and Rudolf Laban -
a tale of choreology and choreography

Dr Valerie Preston-Dunlop

It is Paris, July 1932, backstage at the Théâtre de Champs Elysées. The choreographer of the leading house in Germany, the Berlin Opera Unter den Linden, a man of 52 at the height of his career, is standing waiting. He is visibly overcome. He has witnessed, indeed he has been a member of the international jury which has acclaimed, *La Table verte*. For Rudolf Laban this is not just the occasion for a handshake for the winner of yet another international competition. Rather it is the moment of recognition, for it is Kurt Jooss, his student and collaborator, who has achieved this prize. The winning is not the point. What Jooss has done is to find a new language in which to embody a vision, a language for which both men have searched, but which Laban recognises that Jooss had found. The younger man's talent was always evident, but it had taken twelve years for the layers of craft, the sharpness of social conscience, the astuteness of the aesthetic eye to develop and mesh into the making of the masterpiece *The Green Table*.

Twelve years before in Stuttgart, Kurt had been a music and drama student. It was here that he first encountered Laban, the visionary, revolutionary dance pioneer, twenty years his senior, a formidable personality and man of the world, immersed in researching, creating and writing. In Stuttgart to supervise the publication of his first major book *Die Welt des Tänzers*, Laban gathered around himself, as he had previously done in Munich, in Ascona and in Zürich, individuals drawn by his ideas. Kurt remembered:

> "From the first moment of being in this new world
> a complete change overtook me. I became deeply
> involved, my body changed, and my whole being
> gradually became part of this art." [1]

15

Like Mary Wigman before him, as well as Suzanne Perottet, Käthe Wulff and Dussia Bereska, the direction of Jooss's life was confirmed by the immediate impact of the challenges Laban set himself and which his young colleagues then took upon themselves. He was not alone: Albrecht Knust, later to become the leading scholar of Laban's notation for dance, and before that a valiant fighter for amateur dance; Herta Feist, soon to lead the Laban Berlin School; Jens Keith and Edgar Frank, who became Jooss dancers in Essen, were there too.

What was this "new world"? Laban determined to find the laws of expressive movement. His study of writers as varied as Plato and Freud, and subjects as different as crystallography and anatomy, the skills of fencing, folk dancing and architectural drawing, led him to believe that movement was rule-governed and that its structure, its 'choreological order', could be found. Once found, this would provide the basis for a new form of theatre, the theatre of authentic gesture. This was the new world.

Jooss, already profoundly interested in the production problems of Wagner's opera, entered fully into this search. Laban always needed talented dancers to try out his ideas - Wigman had been just that in 1914. Now it was Jooss's turn, but the opportunities were more fruitful. Mannheim's Nationaltheater took Laban on as guest choreographer for the 1921 season. With the fledgling dancers he created his first major work, *Die Geblendeten* (Illusions), and with the opera dancers created the Bacchanale for Wagner's *Tannhäuser*. This was Jooss's introduction to live dance theatre as a performer, but not one in the traditional sense of dancing movement given him by the choreographer, but with the shared compositional responsibilities which many of Laban's dances entailed.

With the move to Hamburg in 1922, Jooss's role in the Laban circle became clear. He was a leading dancer in the newly-created Tanzbühne Laban - not skilled in alignment, double tours or steps, but in the gesture springing from within - and a budding choreographer, able to finish works started by Laban. He was also a key figure with Dussia Bereska in the choreological research into spatial form in dance (which Laban named choreutics) and, especially of interest to him, into the expressive dynamics of dance, named eukinetics. These two subjects Jooss continued to espouse throughout his career. They were on the curriculum of the Jooss-Leeder School of Dance during his refugee years at Dartington Hall in 1934 - 40, and again at the Folkwanghochschule in the 1950s when he returned to Germany after the second World War.

Choreutics is the study of the complex relationship between the dancer's body and space. Laban was searching for some order in that complexity. He started by naming the space within the dancer's reach the "kinesphere", distinguishing its organisation from that of the stage space or the space shared by other people. He proposed a map, starting from the simple height, breadth and depth concepts that are in the body, progressing to the three planes which are seen in classical dance in the routes of *ports de bras* and *battements*. But, he asked, why do we concentrate on the intersection of the planes, in the familiar positions of the arms in 5th, 2nd and 1st? He proposed the in-between directions to be of equal interest and, since these are oblique, it led to the notion of instability. "Lability" was the name he gave to off balance tilts and leans, so expanding the dance vocabulary. These directions are to be seen in the Old Soldier's walk with Death or in the Mother's reach upstage right in the Refugees' scene.

Choreutics looks at the direct relationship of the dancer with space, not simply moving in it but gathering it in, confronting it, piercing it. Influenced by Schoenberg, who was at that moment abandoning tonal harmonic structures in favour of serialism, Laban searched for principles of harmonics in space. He proposed and practised new "scales" of movement, like those of music, which became fundamental to his training method. These were enlarged *ports de bras* involving the whole body, and weight transference in oblique and off-balance sequences, making great demands on the body's flexibility and stamina. These were danced with one arm dominating, then another, the secondary arm accompanying the first in the "harmonic opposite" direction, often only as far as the elbow. Many times in *The Green Table* this body organisation appears, especially in the women's material.

17

The use of the whole body was a hallmark of the Laban work, in contrast to the isolation found in ballet and some folk dance. Anna Markard's remarks to the dancers of The Birmingham Royal Ballet Company show how she had to adapt their basic coordination to Jooss's. "This is your full concern," she said, of an arm gesture with supporting torso and step. "Your body is all saying one thing ... move within the ribs to reflect the gesture." When posture and gesture are one, the movement is read as authentic, the mover means what he is doing, he is genuinely expressive. This was the hallmark of the expressionistic dance, and Jooss used it in a way tempered by clarity. This authenticity is not always easy to achieve: "Don't qualify the movement for the audience", was a Markard phrase in rehearsal.

Jooss introduced displaced centres theory to achieve greater articulation. The centres from which directional gestures are made can be in the wrist, at the edge of the kinesphere or on the ground. This device may lead to more stylisation or even a grotesque quality. The Profiteer's material - his clap, his movements with the ring from the dead soldier - are examples. What Jooss had absorbed was that spatial organisation is expressive, it provides ways of getting at dance material which conjures character. So he moulded Death spatially, giving him a choreutic structure.

But it was eukinetics which Jooss contributed to and found especially inspiring. It is well known that Laban proposed the basis of the dynamics of expression, eukinetics, as the mixtures of the polar opposites of force, of time, of flow, and of space-in-the-movement. What is less well known is his encounter with the work of Carl Gustav Jung in Zurich in 1916. This provided him with insight into the four psychic ways of functioning identified by Jung and that these manifest themselves in movement not arbitrarily but in a rule-governed way. The connections are between physical function and force, intuitive function and time, mental function and space, emotional function and flow. This insight formed the basis for Laban's profound eukinetic study which Jooss aided and which he uses with clarity in *The Green Table*. The characters have a eukinetic profile which is consistently kept throughout the work. This same theory has been the foundation

18

for Laban-based work with actors and for the now-developed profession of the dance therapist.

What kind of theatre work was Laban doing in this period up to 1928? It was experimental; he was testing every parameter of the traditional role and content of dance. Must it be with music; why not in silence? Why base it on traditional steps; what about dramatic gesture? Why drama; movement itself? Should dancers speak? What is male dance material? Is the soloists/corps de ballet structure an appropriate one for twentieth century dance theatre; the visual grace of ballet is out of sync with society, so what should twentieth-century dance theatre be like? Can dance become literate? Can a new form of social dance be introduced to replace the gap left by the loss of folk dance and the futility and sophistication of current social dance? All these ideas surrounded Jooss. Although he tried his hand as a writer for the Communist Hamburg press in 1923, and led groups in Laban's large movement choirs, he was fundamentally a theatre man. He needed to find a viable movement language for the theatre and to concentrate upon that problem.

In 1924, instead of going on the Tanzbühne Laban European tour Jooss decided to branch out on his own. The Intendant of Münster Opera, Hans Niedecken-Gebhardt, was his contact. He became movement producer there and soon started his own experimental company, the Neue Tanzbühne. A crucial decision was now taken by Jooss. He and his key colleague Sigurd Leeder decided to study ballet, in fact to see their work placed within the traditional proscenium stage, something which Mary Wigman and most Laban followers would never tolerate. Laban had seen himself as a follower in the footsteps of Feuillet and Noverre, but he was also an iconoclast - one has to remember that he had been part of the radical Dada experiments and the alfresco dance happening at Ascona.(c.1916) Jooss was more convergent, feeling the need for clear form, for an accomplished technical vocabulary. His study of ballet in Paris and Vienna equipped him with a clearer understanding of the choices open to him, namely the strength and weaknesses both of the traditional stance of ballet and the experimental Laban-based gesture language of the body.

19

The eight years between Münster and the triumph at the Théâtre de Champs Elysées saw a host of experiences. Jooss, with Leeder, stayed close to Laban for the research and development of a movement notation system, contributing crucial ideas on the writing of timing through his intimate knowledge of music notation. The breakthrough came in the months before, during and immediately after the influential Dancers' Congress of 1927, organised by Laban. Here the various factions of dance were brought together in an effort to promote a united profession (dancers in trade unions). This gathering served as a model for the 1928 Congress, which Jooss organised. The documents of its preparation are revealing. In a letter inviting Niedecken-Gebhardt to cooperate with the dance historian Fritz Böhme, Jooss writes of the need to placate "the three gods - Wigman, Laban and Kröller" (the latter was the influential ballet master of Munich). (Incidentally, Jooss's teacher/student relation to Laban is reflected in his mode of address in correspondence. He is "Herr Laban" and signed "Kurt", while to Niedecken-Gebhardt it is "Liebe Hans".) Jooss made a resounding success of the Congress at which Laban launched his notation system, a triumph with which Jooss and Leeder, Bereska and Knust were keenly and closely associated.

1929 saw Jooss further his career by a move to Essen. He was invited to be director of the dance department at the newly formed High School for the Arts - the Folkwanghochschule. It is significant to note that the dance department was called the Central Laban School, thus moving Laban's professional training headquarters to Essen, under Jooss's leadership, where it became the focus for some twenty-four other Laban schools. Eukinetics, Choreutics and Tanzschrift were on the curriculum but with a balletic influence too. This was the year of Laban's 50th birthday. Every dance magazine brought out a specially congratulatory issue, and a mammoth party was held in Essen, where Jooss's gift to Laban was a ballet, the now well-known *Pavane on the Death of an Infanta* to Ravel's score.

1930 saw the men close again at Bayreuth. Laban (rather surprisingly many thought) had been appointed to Berlin's Opera Unter den Linden after the resignation of Max Terpis. Why not Wigman, or

Kröller? The Wagner Festival was the venue for *Tannhäuser's Bacchanale* again. Jooss's dancers and Laban's Kammertanzers were the performers. Laban received the credit for the choreography with Kurt as assistant. It was certainly a success, but how heavily did Laban rely on Jooss? Was Kurt's skill already outstripping that of his teacher? We really don't know but the suspicion lurks.

Jooss's output of dances was beginning to accelerate. His collaborations with Hein Heckroth (designer) now included Fritz Cohen (composer). The Folkwang Tanzbühne provided his dancers. It was with them that the climactic moment of birth of *The Green Table* was shared.

But what did Jooss take with him from his apprenticeship with Laban? Firstly: the movement of the body as a whole rather than the fragmentation which ballet training produces. Why? Because gesture of the whole body, unified, expresses authenticity of feeling, and that is what both men are after in their works. Secondly: Archetypes. Jooss's protagonists are "the Young Soldier", not Private William; "the Mother", "the Profiteer". Jooss goes beyond Laban, who has his innocent called "the Princess", while Jooss gives us "the Young Girl" in a wartime Brothel, but he does not move to more normal characters, such as Juliet, as does MacMillan. Thirdly: dramatic feeling causing the movement. In ballet at that time, and still now, the steps come first and feeling is, as it were, added on top. But Jooss handled this method better than Laban, for he formed choreographic material for his characters shaped with the metric rhythm of the music, while Laban stayed with the dynamic action, usually in free rhythm.

In 1930, when Jooss re-staged Laban's *Gaukelei*, this process was not complete. His version was still highly expressionistic in style, compared with Auriel von Milloss' version of *Gaukelei* with the Düsseldorf Opera in 1935. The apron strings were loosening but still tied.

Laban's musicless experiments were abandoned by Jooss, but in their stage settings they continued to share the same enjoyment of the minimal - black drapes, mostly. Jooss's costumes have a clear element of realism, reflecting the trend towards objectivity, while

Laban's were more cubist and highly stylised. Some themes of Jooss's dances echo Laban's themes. *The Mirror* and Laban's *Narrenspiegel* (*The Fool's Mirror*) have similarities, and *Chronica* contains the tyrant figure of *Gaukelei*. The Aftermath procession in *The Green Table* was heralded in *Gaukelei* and in the procession of the corpses in *Green Clowns*. The exit of the soldiers after The Farewells uses the spatial canon introduced into Laban's movement choirs. The undercurve and overcurve of weight transference, the successsional and simultaneous flow, the simple use of the three planes, the guidance by surfaces, these are all Laban-derived choreological devices put to excellent use. But more marked than anything is Jooss's use of Laban's eukinetics. He beautifully adapted it to his own theatre style. Both men were convinced that dynamics are the crucial ingredients, the essential way of conveying meaning. For them form grows out of content. So "Death" has a dynamic profile, as has "the Profiteer', and the contrast of "the Young Girl" and "the Mother" is eukinetically formed.

I close with a reference back to history. By 1933 the Ballets Jooss was born and Jooss had become a celebrity. At the same time the National Socialists took office. Jooss emigrated, his school and company were established at Dartington Hall in Devon, and he had tours to the USA, to Europe and elsewhere. For political reasons the two men's paths were not to cross for five years. The bird had flown - but there is a twist in the tail.

Their next meeting was in a poor apartment house. Laban was in Paris again, but in a very different shape from his dapper style of 1932. Having stayed in Germany after the 1933 Nazi election, he had fallen foul of the authorities. At the Berlin Olympic celebrations, the so-called Hitler Games, Laban was dismissed and denied the means to earn. His life's work was reduced to nothing - his notation forbidden, his name erased and his schools shut. He had nine months in isolation at the convent Schloss Banz, then somehow got to Paris, and as a destitute, sick and profoundly depressed man was found some months later by Lisa Ullmann, a teacher in the Jooss School. They could have left him there, but such was Jooss's affection and respect for the man that he fetched him to England and took him into his own family home at Dartington with his wife Aino and daughter Anna. The photographs of the period reveal the extent of Laban's destitution and the sheer humanity of Jooss is evident. Although both men had much more life to lead and work to do, we should leave them there, the younger man at the height of his career, the older in a temporary abyss.

Today's staging of *The Green Table* is evidence again, however, of the fruitful collaboration of these two men, for of Jooss's choreographic output four ballets remain in the repertoire, the four which are written down in Labanotation. Without this score the authentic lineage of the piece would be in danger. That *The Green Table* can be staged is a memorial to the pioneering work in choreology and choreography of both Laban and Jooss.

Notes

[1] Kurt Jooss, '*Mein bisheriger Lebenslauf*'. Mss. Essen, November 1927, Jooss-Archiv, Amsterdam. Quoted in Anna and Hermann Markard, *Jooss* (Köln: Ballett-Bühnen-Verlag, 1985), p. 29.

The Green Table in context, an examination of *The Green Table* in its political, economic and artistic context
Dr Clare Lidbury

The Green Table is very much a product of its time. It draws on the general feelings of the period and on the particular experiences of the choreographer. Jooss's artistic activity in the post-war period took place against a background of political, social and economic devastation. The end of World War I in the September of 1918 left Germany with severe problems - over one and a half million Germans were dead and nearly four million were wounded. The cost, in materials, lost talent, despair, injured and sick minds, was incalculable, while in addition, Germany was virtually without any form of government or economic policy, with improvement very slow in coming.

It is difficult to assess to what extent Jooss was affected by the situation. At the end of the war Jooss was only 17 so did not experience life in military service himself, but one of his brothers had been killed in action. As a thinking, feeling individual he would have observed the aftermath - despair, physical mutilation, agony of mind - and witnessed the return to economic and political stability. Indeed the economic recovery in the early 1920s coincided with Jooss's work with Laban's group and his own touring company - Zwei Tanzer. The economic recovery that allowed industry to thrive also allowed municipalities and states who ran the theatres to use foreign loans to support their activities. These subsidised theatres existed all over Germany, employing many dancers and choreographers - as well as musicians, singers, designers and directors. Jooss, working at the subsidised theatres in Münster and Essen, would undoubtedly have benefited from the improving economic climate.

However, as the economic situation worsened at the end of the 1920s, so the theatre was affected as much as any other institution in the country. Many dancers became unemployed:

"After the wandering unemployed singers and
musicians which one has seen giving concerts in
the streets of Berlin, one now finds dancers in this
pitiable role."[1]

As Jooss's work at Essen was divided between the theatre and the
Folkwangschule, he would have met with financial difficulties in both
areas. Indeed, we know that when Jooss wanted to attend the *Grand
Concours de Chorégraphie* July of 1932, which he of course won, he
had to beg the money to travel from a variety of sources. Today, no
doubt, we would call this sponsorship.

There are various ways in which the creation of *The Green Table*
was affected by the economic situation. First it is known that Fritz
Cohen wanted to write for a larger orchestra than the sixteen piece
orchestra provided by the organisers of the *Grand Concours de
Chorégraphie*. Cohen was told that he could have as large an orchestra as he wanted but that the company would have to pay for any extra
players. After this Cohen changed direction completely and wrote the
music, most successfully, for two pianos only. We can also see that the
designs for the table and for the costumes were kept extremely simple. For example, when the women change from Refugees to
Prostitutes (for scene VI), they do not have a complete change of costume, but merely take off their head scarves and loosen their hair,
adding belts with gauze flowers. This simple transition transforms the
women completely. Perhaps the clearest evidence of the economic situation, however, is seen in the Gentlemen in Black. The reason that
the masks were used in the opening and closing scenes was to dis-
guise the female members of the company. Der Ballett der Stadt
Essen only had sixteen dancers, and it could not afford to employ any
others to replace the women around the table. Incidentally, of course,
the masks are remarkably effective, helping to portray the characters
of the Gentlemen in Black. Thus, out of necessity we see inventive
and very effective answers to economic problems.

The effect of the political situation on Jooss's work is harder to

were strong political rumblings throughout the late
ly 1930s of which Jooss was acutely aware. His reading
ne, a liberal political journal, kept him abreast of what
was really happening, so he could not have been surprised when in
1933 the Nazification of culture began with the establishment of the
Reichskulturkammer. This had a special branch for gymnastics and
dance, directed by Rudolf Bode, a eurythmy teacher. The principles
for the Art of Dance, as defined by Nazi policy, were laid down in an
article published by Bode in the periodical *Musik* (August 1933),
entitled *Die Bedetung der Korperlichen Bewegung Für die Erneuerung
der deutschen Kultur* (The Importance of Body Movement for the
Renewal of German Body Culture). This included such statements
as:- instead of the 'artificial artist' - the highly trained, finely tuned
artist - the ordinary person with unspoiled and instinctive responses
was to be preferred; that all movement was to be accompanied by
sound, with music and gesture equally important (music was not to be
mere accompaniment); also, all movement was to be rhythmic; all
movement was to be comprehensible to the untrained observer, to be
'movement of the people'.

This would suggest that the art of dance in Germany was not to
come from the theatre but from the people. Clearly Jooss, with his
roots firmly in the theatre and with a highly trained, technically proficient company, could not be a party to such thinking. Lewitan suggested that Bode's ideas were "evidently spoken by a non-dancer
having but a small idea of our art," [2] continuing:

> "It is a matter of fact that those ideas are to
> become basic in Germany in the education of
> dancers, and therefore it is necessary to know them
> and to adopt them"[3]

It is clear why Jooss would have found the ideas unacceptable. To
have such limitations forcibly imposed on a creative artist in the theatre would have been intolerable.

The rise of Nazism with its anti-Jewish policy was an additional problem for Jooss. In March 1933, Fritz Cohen and two other company members were discharged from employment by the municipality. However, by this time the Ballets Jooss were under private management and thus free from Nazi policy administered by the state; Jooss continued to fight for the rights of his Jewish, half-Jewish and quarter-Jewish company members.

A newspaper editorial from 1933 contained a lengthy tirade against Jooss, confirming that he was unable and unwilling to adopt the principles of the new German Art of Dance and that his continued support of non-Arians was a dangerous line for Jooss to pursue:

> "He pretends not to be able to fulfil his artistic mission without Cohen the Jew: a strange comment for a so-called innovator of the German Dance.
> Should this attitude of Jooss's not have taught us long ago to see what kind of truth lies in this "German" dance art originated by Jooss?! Was the scandal in the Paris Music Hall, where he demonstrated his "German awareness" not enough to give this gentleman the sack, allowing him to fulfil his artistic mission elsewhere where no consideration for Germanism is required? For quite incomprehensible reasons...it was thought that Jooss should be treated differently to other persons who repudiate the principles of the people and nation and his wishes be granted beyond all limits...Such things may have been possible in the field of art formerly, in the morbid era abandoned by all good spirits, and infected by Jewish and liberalistic art snobbery which spread throughout our German fatherland. In the new Germany the artist has the damned duty to exercise spiritual and national discipline due to his public mission." [4]

Jooss clearly was not adhering to required political policy. His refusal to submit to the Nazi regime was a dangerous, if courageous, stand to take. In September 1933, as a consequence of this increasing political pressure and activity, Jooss and his company left Germany for good. He, like many others (Gropius, Brecht, Weill, Hindemith, the list is almost endless) found that he could no longer live or work under Nazi rule.

*   *   *   *   *

In looking at Jooss in relation to other choreographers and the state of dance in general, we find that Germany was in a rather different situation from the rest of Europe, for, outside Germany, Modern Dance was rarely the most important dance form. In France, with the ex-Ballet Russe choreographers Nijinska, Lifar and Balanchine, ballet was the main focus. In Britain, de Valois and Rambert were fostering the talents of Ashton and Tudor while alternative dance forms were offered by, amongst others, the Margaret Morris Movement, the revived Greek Dance of Ruby Ginner and the work of Margaret Barr at Dartington Hall. In the USSR, ballet was of course the major dance form, but things were changing even here. In 1927, Russia saw its first 'revolutionary ballet' - *The Red Poppy* - which became a turning point in Russian ballet leading the way to other works with contemporary themes.

In Germany, in spite of rising unemployment and galloping inflation, a great number of theatres and opera houses still provided employment for many dancers, choreographers and ballet masters. Jooss was just one of many working in the state theatres of small towns. If they were not pupils of Laban, most of the other dancers working in Germany probably were, or had been, pupils of Mary Wigman - such as Harald Kreutzberg, Grete Palucca, Yvonne Georgi and Max Terpis.

In addition there were 'independent' dancer/choreographers - the communist Hans Weidt, for example, Berthe Trumpy, Valeska Gert,

Vera Skoronel and many more. Evidence of the flourishing of Modern Dance is seen in the growth of the German Dancers' Congresses. By 1930 at the third Congress held in Munich, 1400 participants were involved. Over the seven day event performances were given by the groups of Rosalie Chladek, Jutta Klamt, Vera Skoronel, Dorothee Günther and Maya Lex, Gret Palucca, Jooss and many others, including companies from the United States, Holland, Denmark, Poland, Hungary, Yugoslavia and Czechoslovakia. [5]

Rather differently and completely independently, Oskar Schlemmer, at The Bauhaus, was doing interesting work in dance. It is known that Rudolf Laban and Oskar Schlemmer served together on the Committee for the Magdeburg Dance Congress of 1927 and that: "each was aware and respectful of each other's work". [5] The Bauhaus foundation course (*vorkus*) explored the three basic geometric forms of triangle, square and circle, and the primary colours 'emotionally' and 'spiritually' connected with each - respectively yellow, red and blue. Clear links can be made here with the parallel thinking of Laban - and Jooss - in their exploration of the basic designs and dimensions, and the dynamics (the colour) inherent in the forms. Schlemmer explored the relationship between people and the space around them and was not concerned with the people as bodies or as human forms, but more as puppets or 'beings' in space. In effect Jooss and Schlemmer were starting from opposite points. Jooss started with the content - what the dance was to express - and worked outwards with the content shaping the form. Schlemmer started with the form and allowed it to shape the content of his ritualistic, unreal, almost architectural characters.

*   *   *

It is at this point that we must remember that Jooss was not just a choreographer but a man of the theatre. He was an actor and director and he must have been aware of the developments in theatre that were taking place during the 1920s and 30s. Expressionism, the

29

rejection of accepted aesthetic standards in an attempt to present externally the inner experience, was, of course, not confined to the art world, but influenced all forms of theatre. Jooss, like many dancers of the period, joined in the search for new ideas, particularly while working with Laban, crying out against inherited artistic concepts and values. Jooss himself said "[in] the Expressionist dance in Germany one did not need great proficiency: strong intensity was all convincing." [7] While many continued to rebel against those concepts by seeking to reveal their soul and inner emotions in formless out-pouring of movement, Jooss moved towards a more structured form of dance with technically proficient dancers and with presentation and theatricality as important as the ideas put into dance - Jooss's work was "dance-theatre".

Expressionism was comparatively short-lived, but long-lasting in its effect. It was a catalyst for releasing artists from accepted practises and aesthetics, enabling them to explore new pathways and ideas, in all the arts. This freedom, once gained, was not to be easily lost. Jooss had been exposed to Expressionism during his formative, creative years while working with Laban. However, his strong social awareness and satirical comment together with his neutral, "undecorated" approach makes his work closer to the post-Expressionist trend of the *Neue Sachlichkeit* than to Expressionism itself.

There is no direct translation for *Neue Sachlichkeit*, it usually being termed 'New Objectivity' or 'new matter-of-factness'. As with Expressionism, the term was first coined in the art world for an exhibition prepared during 1923-25. *Neue Sachlichkeit* may be seen as being both an off-shoot of and a reaction against Expressionism. Willett suggests that what had changed "was not so much the principles and formal innovations arrived at from 1910 onwards, as the spirit in which they were applied." [8] What in Expressionism had been ecstatic, loud, dynamic and subjective in the *Neue Sachlichkeit* trend became sober, quiet, static and objective. This objectivity was the key factor - seeing the world as it actually was, with neutrality and a matter-of-factness, with utility and an absence of decoration. It was also an attempt to make comment on topical, social issues. Jooss relates to these ideas of social comment and topicality in his work, as well as to the idea of utility - seen in the lack of stage decoration and in his absence of ornamentation of movement (no virtuosity or unnecessary decoration).

To a certain extent then, Jooss was still challenging the accepted aesthetics of classical dance as the Expressionists had done, for his work is not "ballet" in the accepted sense. He had, however, moved beyond Expressionism to a more disciplined approach in his creativity, and to a much wider scope, principally in the topicality of his subject matter. These aspects of his work, combined with his awareness of the society in which he lived, clearly place Jooss within the *Neue Sachlichkeit* trend.

At the same time it may be seen that Jooss's work paralleled in dance the work that Stanislavsky was doing in the theatre. The idea that a dancer should think himself in to his role, that he should have motivations for all the movements that he makes and be aware of his relationship to the total event are all fundamental to Jooss's working practice and clearly link to the theories of Stanislavsky. Similarly we might look at *The Green Table* and some aspects of Brecht's ideas - the episodic nature of the work, the delineation of characters as types rather than as named individuals, in the ballet's subject matter and particularly in the way some characters in the ballet are presented so that we as an audience are not caught up in their plight but are able to observe passively the situation in which we see them.

Brecht and Jooss were working on opposite sides of the country - Brecht in Berlin and Jooss in Essen. We know that Jooss went to Berlin to see *The Threepenny Opera*, but does not seem to have acknowledged any debt to Brecht's ideas. Rather then, what is important, is that both men were moving on from the accepted aesthetics of the theatre, from their roots in Expressionism, to finding their own forms and styles. It is really not so surprising that in that time and at that stage in their careers, that we should be able to observe similarities between the work of these two men.

*   *   *

31

So far I have given an overview of the political, economic and artistic climate in which Jooss was working at the beginning of the 1930s. When we look specifically at *The Green Table* we see that certain key images are very much part of a general satirical, anti-establishment feeling prevailing at the time. For example, Jooss was not alone in depicting Death as a skeleton, for it had been a popular image during the First World War and immediately afterwards. [9] Jean Weber's *Face to Face* (1917) shows a soldier in a trench face to face with Death - a crouching skeleton - leering over the top. Louis Raemaeker's *The Harvest* of 1914 shows a huge skeletal 'Death the Reaper', harvesting tiny soldiers as if they were endless fields of corn. This image of Death as a skeleton was not new in 1914 for it had first been popularised during the Middle Ages - as in the Lübeck *Totentanz* or Holbein's *Dance of Death.*

Similarly Jooss's image of Death as a God of war, a centurion-like figure, was also depicted in art of the time. L. J. Jordaan's *At the Beginning of the Peace conference* (1907), for example, shows a huge figure of Death as a Centurion bending down towards a tiny naked figure clutching the white flag of surrender. The image of Death as a war machine was also popular - Jordaan's *The Robot* (c.1917) presents an enormous mechanical figure striding over cowering soldiers, futilely shooting at it. Kubin's *Der Kreig* (1915) brings these images of Death together in the one work. The striding figure is similar to Jordaan's robot - the naked body with clearly visible bone structure relates to the skeleton images while the shield, fighting implement and helmet suggests the Centurion image.

Likewise, the peace conference had been a popular satirical image from slightly earlier in the century. *Le Caricature de la Conference de la Paix* published in 1908 was a volume of prints of cartoons from major European countries, published to coincide with the Second International Peace Conference. *The Medal of the Peace Conference* published in the volume shows five people clearly of different nationalities sitting round a table. The 'front' of the medal shows smiling congenial faces. The 'back' of the medal shows the delegates clasping their weapons. This satirises the fact that many of the nations represented at the conference were also spending huge amounts of money on re-arming themselves. Arthur Young's *Having Their Fling* goes one step further, suggesting that the entire establishment was in on the war business together, by depicting four capitalists - politicians or financiers - jumping for joy while a battle takes place in the background. The satirical cartoon is perhaps taken to its extreme in the work of George Grosz.

As might be expected, much literature of the period deals with experiences of those involved in the conflict of 1914-1918. Perhaps the most revealing is Erich Maria Remarque's *All Quiet on the Western Front,* written from the point of view of the soldier. We read of his day-to-day existence, of fighting, death, fear, of his relationship with his Mother and his horror of saying good-bye to her. At that particular time - when Germany had just recovered from one catastrophic war but was preparing to rush into a second - the soldiers' discussion, about why war happens at all, is particularly pertinent:

> "Then what exactly is war for?" asks Tjaden. Kat shrugs his shoulders. "There must be some people to whom the war is useful."
>
> "Well I'm not one of them," grins Tjaden.
>
> "Not you nor anyone else here."
>
> "Who are they then?" persists Tjaden. "It isn't any use to the Kaiser either. He has everything he can want already."
>
> "I'm not so sure about that," contradicts Kat, "he has not had a war up till now. And every full-grown emperor requires at least one war, otherwise he wouldn't be famous. You look in your school books."
>
> "And generals too," adds Detering, "they become famous through war."
>
> "Even more famous than emperors," adds Kat.

> "There are other people back behind there
> ho profit from war, that's certain," growls
> etering.
> "I think it is more of a kind of fever," says
> Albert. "No one in particular wants it, and then all
> at once there it is. We didn't want the war, the oth-
> ers say the same thing - and yet half the world is in
> it all the same."[10]

This passage, in its naive questioning of the necessity for war, seems to relate exactly to the antics of the Gentlemen in Black - they need the war as a means of justifying their existence. None of the other characters in the ballet need the war but they are caught up in it, some willingly like the recruited soldiers and some unwillingly, like the Mother and the Young Girl.

So far we have an outline of the artistic climate in which Jooss was working and to which he contributed. We cannot know whether any of these images directly influenced Jooss, although it seems like-ly that the stance of Kubin's figure did influence that one move in Death's dance, for the similarities are too strong to be ignored. The other images of Death were constantly being used by artists of the time and it seems that Jooss was absorbing and transforming them for his own purposes. What is suggested here is that Jooss was acutely aware of current opinions and feelings and that he both capitalised on and contributed greatly to that popular opinion through the creation of his own important works of art - not just *The Green Table* but also in *The Big City* and *The Mirror*, for example.

It is possible also to see Jooss drawing upon influences from his early creative years for we see particular aspects of Expressionism in *The Green Table*, specifically in the more grotesque elements of the ballet - in the concept of Death as a character personified and dressed as a skeleton or, even more overtly grotesque perhaps, in his make up, with black eyes, black angular cheeks, black tip of nose and black lips contrasted with white high lighted cheek bones, white

chin and white nose markings, all making a rather bizarre and dis-
torted face. This grotesqueness is seen also in the masks of the
Gentlemen in Black with the exaggeration of certain features - eye-
brows or foreheads for example.

Perhaps Jooss was also inspired by the work of other practitioners
of his time. One practitioner who declared that he had influenced
Jooss's creation of *The Green Table*, was Oskar Schlemmer, with his
claim that the ballet was "inspired in part by the Bauhaus Dance
Tours of the late 1920s." [11] As there is little in common between the
working methods of the two men, it seems likely that any inspiration
would have come from visual images. Indeed, pictures of
Schlemmer's *Faschung* (1928) show a table, end-on to the audience,
with various masked characters sitting on chairs around the table and
sitting on the table itself, in a range of poses and attitudes. It is possible to see that this might have been an image which Jooss drew upon
in his creation of the first scene. However, we do not know if Jooss
saw Schlemmer's ballet, or any photographs, and so it is possible that
any similarities may be purely coincidental.

Finally we come to images that Jooss acknowledged were influencing factors in the creation of *The Green Table*. The first of these is
the Lübeck *Totentanz* which Jooss saw as a young man. The idea of
Death dancing with people from different walks of life was first
worked on by Jooss and Leeder during 1926-27. This dance was set
aside when Jooss was forced by injury to stop dancing, but it was an
idea that Jooss continued to work with. In fact at the time of the competition he was working on a solo based on the Dance of Death. As
the rules of the competition demanded a group work his solo was
obviously inappropriate, but Jooss was so involved in the solo that,
"he could not tear his mind and creative longing away from this artistic compulsion."[12] So, Jooss attempted to expand the solo into a
group work.

Jooss also acknowledged that his memories of the first world War
became a part of The Farewells:

"Our house was on a slope...about a hundred yards down was a cross-roads. On that day I saw all the men with horses - you know artillery, the guns...makes a terrific rattling noise. Nothing could be heard, only the shouts of the soldiers with their horses rattling...The Farewells...is exactly that first day of war with the rattling guns... military behaviour... farewell scenes and soldiers in training" [13]

We know also that Jooss's playing of Zeus and the Bull in Kaiser's *Europa* at the Dusseldorf Spielhaus in 1930 was an influencing factor:

"I must make a ballet where I can play such a beast [because] it's wonderful...The bull became the way to the figure of Death in *The Green Table*." [14]

Another influential factor was *Die Weltbühne*, probably:

"the most influential journal of opinion in Germany...*Die Weltbühne* tried to inform rather than incite and to guide liberal readers gently towards pacifism and socialist reform". [15]

In the late 1920s it was edited by the pacifist Carl von Ossietzky. One of the main writers was the political journalist Kurt Tucholsky, "a very great man" [16] who influenced Jooss's political thinking around the time of the final conception of *The Green Table*:

"Don't believe it, don't believe it, these peace talks. It's all rubbish, it's all fake, they are secretly preparing a new war." [17]

36

These forecasts, together with Jooss's memories of the Great War, his previous work on the Dance of Death, his performance of The Bull, the original influence of the Lübeck *Totentanz*, his work with Laban and the general political and artistic atmosphere of that time, somehow all came together, were assimilated and absorbed, and were formed into *The Green Table*.

Sixty years on the ballet remains as pertinent as ever although our current political, economic and artistic climate is very different from the one in which Jooss was working. Jooss composed many other ballets, some of which also reflected his strong social and political consciousness. However, it is *The Green Table* which remains his masterpiece, speaking across time to all who see it.

Notes

[1] Horst Koegler, *In the Shadow of the Swastika* (New York: Dance Perspectives Foundation, 1974), p. 28.

[2] Joseph Lewitan, 'The Dance in New Germany', *The Dancing Times* (September 1933), p. 565.

[3] *Ibid.* p. 567.

[4] Anonymous newspaper article quoted by Anna and Hermann Markard, *Jooss.* (Koln: Ballett-Bühnen-Verlag, 1985), p. 51.

[5] Horst Koegler, *In the Shadow of the Swastika* (New York: Dance Perspectives Foundation, 1974), p. 18.

[6] Debra McCall, 'Reconstructing Schlemmer's Bauhaus Dances' in Arnold L.Lehman and Brenda Richardson, (Editors) *Oskar Schlemmer*, Exhibition Catalogue (The Baltimore Museum of Art, 1986), p. 150.

[7] Anna and Hermann Markard, *Jooss* (Koln: Ballett-Bühnen-Verlag, 1985), p. 31.

[8] John Willett, *Expressionism* (London: Weidenfeld and Nicholson, 1970) p. 192.

[9] D.J.R.Bruckner and others, *Art Against War* (New York: Abbeville Press, 1984.)

[10] Erich Maria Remarque, *All Quiet on the Western Front* (London: P.G.Putnam's Sons, 1929), pp. 224-225.

[11] Debra McCall, 'Reconstructing Schlemmer's Bauhaus Dances' in Arnold L.Lehman and Brenda Richardson, (Editors) *Oskar Schlemmer*, Exhibition Catalogue (The Baltimore Museum of Art, 1986), p. 150.

[12] Walter Terry, 'How a Ballet was Born', *World Journal Tribune* (March 1967).

[13] Transcription of a tape recorded interview between Kurt Jooss and Tobi Tobias for the Oral History Project, The Dance Collection, New York Public Library. September 1976.

[14] Michael Huxley, '*The Green Table* - A Dance of Death' *Ballett International* (August /September 1982), p. 8.

[15] Wolf von Eckardt and Salman L.Gilman, *Bertholt Brecht's Berlin* (London: Abelard, 1976), p. 47.

[16] Transcription of a tape recorded interview between Kurt Jooss and Tobi Tobias for the Oral History Project, The Dance Collection, New York Public Library. September 1976.

[17] *Ibid.*

Tension and intention, form and feeling: an investigation of Jooss's use of rhythm and dynamics in *The Green Table*

Andy Adamson

An examination of the eukinetic aspects of Jooss's work provides us with the means for describing and discussing the dynamics and rhythm of movement, which so often give dance its sense of vitality and variety. Predominantly this paper addresses eukinetic issues since I believe that it is this area of Jooss's work that makes it so distinctive. Of course what really makes him different is that he demonstrates an understanding of both choreutics and eukinetics. His work is full of dynamic and rhythmic elements, but shows an equal concern for clarity and appropriateness of body design. He uses trace forms, pathways and relationships, both between dancers, between the dancer and his/her environment and between dancer and spectator. However, this paper will confine itself to a discussion of eukinetics, since this is the element most at risk in restagings of Jooss's ballets in those instances where dancers do not have training or experience in the use of Jooss's dance language.

The language of dance has at its root certain fundamentals which can be understood by all humans, since everyone:

a) is affected by gravity and may choose to indulge in or resist that force;

b) has a pulse-rate which is governed by emotional or physical situations;

c) must draw breath in a rhythmical manner .

These three common factors lie at the root of our body language.

The Jooss-Leeder language observes the way in which human movement is governed by these natural laws and provides theatre practitioners with the necessary tools to relate the inner impulses of thought or feeling to the outward forms and actions of the body. We

39

commonly talk about feeling relaxed, or being a bit uptight, as states of mind, when what we are actually describing is a muscular response to gravity.

The body's natural impulses to move usually stem from the need to produce tension to overcome the force of gravity, or sometimes relaxing and yielding to give in to that force. Often the movement will stem from the desire to satisfy some need, perhaps to greet a friend, to run away in fear, or to search for food. In each case a motivation precedes the movement - an intention leads to the necessary body tension required to perform the movement. These intentions can arise so instinctively that we barely notice them. We go about our daily actions in a way which is intuitive or, more often, habitual. Often without knowing it, our emotional selves will respond to the varying tensions and relaxations of our body. For example, in a situation which is stressful the body is likely to tighten, the result is that we feel stressed; or if we allow our muscles to give in to the pull of gravity while continuing to go about our work, then the result may be a feeling of lethargy or even depression. Laban, Jooss and Leeder all recognized that these varying tensions and relaxations (and varying responses to the force of gravity) were the very stuff of movement and could be moulded into dance, dance which is then capable of revealing something of our inner state of mind.

Natural rhythms, arising from activity of the heart (pulse) and breathing mechanism, give a sense of pattern or structure to these tensions and relaxations. Sudden gasps for breath or sudden exhalations can create very emotionally charged movement. Responding to a fast pulse can produce a sense of excitement or agitation, while a slow pulse can seem ponderous, or easy going. In work, rhythm performance can aid with repetition of tasks, perhaps helping to make them more pleasurable. Actions seem to make more sense when they have a definite beginning middle or end. If we remove all rhythmic stress from our movement we may observe in even the most mundane of actions that the subtle placement of accents has a role to play.

In rhythmic terminology Jooss-Leeder sees an impulse as something quite specific, it is a movement with an initial accent, an explosion (large or small) with no preparation, and which gradually dissipates its energy. In motivation terms a true impulse comes as a surprise or a shock; a sudden realisation or a spur of the moment decision. Its opposite, an impact, is a movement with a terminal accent, something that comes to a definite end. A series of impacts may seek to emphasize a point, to impress, or even shock. If an action is prepared for, executed, then followed through, a movement with a transitional accent may be observed - preparation, accent, follow through. Performed with the assistance of gravity this can result in a swinging, pendulum-like movement. Such movement can be fun, look at the child in the playground, the sensation of swinging gives pleasure. However, it can also give us power - performed with high energy it can harness the force of gravity to give greater strength or uplift, while a low energy swing may appear hypnotic.

Besides shaping our actions rhythmically, we also subject our movements to more or less control, binding or freeing the flow of motion. We speak about Bound flow or Free flow, Guided or Unguided movement. This may imply something about the care with which you wish to perform an action. An attempt to protect yourself from injury is likely to produce Bound flow, as would any movement requiring intricate or detailed action. But a more abandoned attitude would produce free flowing, uncontained movement leading to a sense of fun or perhaps being out of control. This could be either pleasurable or frightening. It's also to do with the extent to which the individual is prepared "to go with the flow". So, through varying tensions and relaxations, weights and strengths, by intuitively placing rhythmic stresses, and by choosing how much control to exercise, we give purpose, clarity and meaning to our movements.

The Jooss-Leeder language observes these natural laws and thus provides the perfect medium for a theatre practitioner concerned with the human condition. Jooss was just such a person. Jooss clearly felt that *The Green Table* was not a political ballet, that it could never change anybody.[1] What he was interested in might be described as 'the plight of human misery', the suffering that people had gone through. He was interested in all the facets of humanity, indeed his

41

great gift was that he could reveal to us this 'plight' through comedy as well as tragedy. He presents us with the face of laughter and of tears, masterfully juxtaposing one with another to produce genuine moments of pathos. Although his characters are unnamed and may stand as archetypes they appear as though individuals. Their faces are recognisable as those of real people, with real desires, with real emotions, yet the spectator sees only the motions. It's not possible to see the actual intention for movement, only the tensions produced by the bodies of the dancers as a result. It is the spectator who must interpolate and interpret meaning by providing the link between the visible tensions of the dancers' bodies and the impulses which lead to them,

In *The Green Table* we can see the careful articulation of movement built around these natural laws, movement that unfolds and develops in an organic way. *The Green Table* offers a wealth of examples in which characters convey to us their inner feeling through the rhythm and dynamic of their actions. The Gentlemen in Black, for example, is a scene full of diplomatic rhetoric. Social decorum is maintained throughout, despite apparent opposing viewpoints. Lightness and bound flow show the measure of self control of which these Gentlemen are capable. But there is ever present the threat of impending violence. Politeness and lightness are juxtaposed with emphatically presented individual statements, conveyed through strong impacted gestures.

Jooss described Cohen's music for this scene, a rather sardonic tango, as like café music in the background, seemingly overheard through some open window of the conference room.[2] Indeed, although the movements of the Gentlemen in Black coincide with the music, the rhythm of the music and dance seem to run along two parallel lines. They are independent yet intertwined. The dance has its own musicality, carefully constructed from eukinetic elements. The scene opens with the lightest of initial accents and a series of group tableaux follows, each articulated with a terminal accent. For the first eight bars, movement is entirely in the light area of the dynamic spectrum. There then follows a section placing greater emphasis on individuality. Three of the Gentlemen express their points of view through gestures which slap the table. Three different postures suggesting three different ideas, yet linked by a common rhythmic identity. The gesture made by the third Gentleman is echoed by the others on his side of the table. The sequence of three impacts plus echoing fourth is immediately repeated at double speed, giving yet greater strength to these emphatic gestures. Four bars of lighter dynamics seem to diffuse the building tension, but immediately we are plunged into a sequence of stronger and often impacted movements. Strength and building tension is further emphasized by jumps and by movement away from and onto the table itself. In a unison statement, implying common aggression, they surge at one another to perform a 'handstand' jump (hands on the table), then jump away pas de chat-like, before lunging back at one another. Yet again the tension is diffused into lightness, but soon builds again in conflict. A pseudo sword fight ensues, but the Gentlemen are incapable of coming to blows, (the two sides never actually make physical contact) and return to the conference table, resuming their opening positions. The first eight bars of lightness are recapitulated, almost as though they are marking time as a prelude to the culminating sequence of aggressiveness. Lines are drawn for battle. Guns are drawn for conflict. But at the last moment these are raised above their heads - then fired! Is the gunshot an impact? Certainly the sound we hear makes its' impact. But the action of the bullet flying from the gun is impulsive, the initiation for the scenes of death and misery that are to follow.

The Farewells is the first of six scenes sandwiched between prologue and epilogue. We are introduced to the protagonists, each with an identifiable character, and each of whom demonstrate their various responses to the call of the Standard Bearer to go to war. The Young Soldier bursts onto the scene, you don't even see him take off, he's just there in mid-air. His forward surging, impulsive action thrusts him toward his objective of honour and glory, symbolized by the flag, which he acknowledges with a strongly impacted pose. The attack of his movement seems to generate the impulsive run of the Young Girl, who follows him in. His body remains alert and uplifted, ready for action. She tenderly tries to restrain him, first by using her weight, then folding her body in towards him with a soft impulse initiated from her abdomen. But to no avail, and the young man falls under the spell of the flag, his movements reduced to a lifeless repetition of marching on the spot, accompanied by hypnotically swinging arm movements.

The Old Soldier enters with the burden of responsibility, his steps are heavier than the other soldiers and his movement hindered by the two women to whom he is joined. They seem to impede him with their body weight and convey to us their unwillingness that he goes to war. He summons his strength and takes centre stage, but in doing so, as he comes forward, you sense his hesitancy. He is not absolutely convinced that this is the right thing to do. His walk is punctuated by a stopping, impacted action. Nevertheless he takes centre stage and as he raises his arms in an image of crucifixion you know that he's prepared to make the ultimate sacrifice. The Woman, presumably his wife, with strong twisting gestures, seems to be crying out in anger or frustration. The Mother, with a sense of weight, suspends herself from his arm. A feeling of despair is conveyed, which disappears as she lifts and floats up, perhaps in prayer. The Woman collapses to the ground and then tenderly rises to bid farewell. As the soldiers march mindlessly at the bidding of The Standard Bearer, each of the three women protagonists is presented with a different movement motif, involving speed and dynamic. The Young Girl seems the weakest of the three. Her motif runs lightly forward, reaching for the Young Soldier, then hesitates, turning, in an imagined embrace. The Woman, stronger and more determined, leaps toward the soldiers, then dances backwards, alongside them, as if to prevent their leaving. As the soldiers come under the shadow of Death their bodies lose strength and they pass heavily beneath his outstretched arms. Only the Woman runs defiantly past him. The Mother, who has moved slowly and limply, hesitates as she catches sight of Death, moves quickly after the soldiers as if to warn, then slowly approaches Death, perhaps in fear, perhaps to plead. the Young Girl collapses under the threatening gaze of the Profiteer.

In The Battle the soldiers confront us with a real show of strength. Both they and their civilized counterparts, the Gentlemen in Black, work always with great rhythmic variety. Impact, impulse and swing are all present. Whereas the Gentlemen have danced with lightness and a kind of light strength, the soldiers demonstrate full strength, articulated by powerful accents. In a natural and organic way an impact can give rise to an impulse (Newton's cradle) or meld together to become a swing. In The Battle an impacted movement often becomes the impulse for the subsequent movement, as in Newton's third law - to every action there is an equal and opposite reaction. For example, as the Standard Bearer jumps into the centre of a group of soldiers he lands with strong terminal accent (impact). This in turn produces a reaction from the soldiers which is explosive, like a grenade going off (impulse). We see these two things as though they were one. The Battle may be seen as a parallel with the Prologue. But here there is physical contact where previously there has been none; here there is strength that previously was only hinted at; now things get out of control and lose balance (free flow) when previously they were stopped just before control was lost.

After the storm of The Battle, The Refugees seems to offer a moment of calm. But in fact this scene is very much about turbulence. A group of people uprooted and flung into the unknown, and an old woman (the Mother) struggling with death, but finally accepting it as blissful release. Jooss makes these points all the more poignantly for the use of understatement. Pastel shades of dynamic changes are made, with energy levels rarely more than a loud whisper.

From the first moments of this scene we register the unity of the group. They share a common quiet dynamic, with all movements performed with bound flow. A background of unaccented, sustained movement is maintained by the main group of women, as the Mother gradually emerges as solo figure. Her movement becomes much more varied, in contrast to the women, with phrases of sharply punctuated poses alternating with scurrying or lilting movement. As the whole group moves in unison again, a subtle sense of weight is achieved through use of undercurve in the travelling step. Death emerges slowly from his hiding place in the downstage left corner, causing the women to halt abruptly and start in fright, then flee the stage, leaving the Young Girl and the Mother alone with Death.

In The Partisan Jooss draws together various eukinetic features to highlight the complexity of the Woman's dilemma. The entire section is built around the use of opposite polarities — impactive versus impulsive movement, free versus bound flow, stable versus labile movement, fast versus slow movement. This emphasis on opposites makes the drama of the situation all the more evident. Jooss shapes the movement rhythmically in order to expose something of the Woman's crisis. Her impacted movements are usually her most decisive while her inner turmoil finds expression in movements of an impulsive nature. Her indecision and precariousness of situation are further emphasized by contrasting solid and stable moments with labile, off-balance movements of the whole body. This, combined with the use of free and bound flow movement, helps to convey the degree of control that the Woman exercises over her situation. It is as if Jooss wants us to see into her mind as she struggles to come to terms with the difficult decision to take a human life. As Death and the Soldiers appear, to take revenge for the Woman's deed, using ingredients which individually are simple walking patterns, Jooss weaves a complex rhythmic counterpoint.

Jooss's treatment of the Partisan is eukinetically varied and complex. But it is the figure of Death himself who undergoes the most striking dynamic and rhythmic metamorphosis of all the protagonists. Most of the time we register his gestures as strong, either impactive and punchy or sustained and crushing giving us a clear image of Death as a figure of great power. In his solo all the landings of his jumps are done with tremendous weight. However throughout the ballet his tensions change to fit the situation in which he finds himself. Our first impression is indeed as a figure all powerful, pressing, carving, crushing and hammering his way through space. The repeated use of impacted movement together with a tremendous sense of weight in everything he does helps to convey his relentlessness and that every living thing must ultimately find its end (impact) in death. In The Farewells it is Death who calls the tune, beating out the rhythm incessantly. In The Battle again he becomes the Slayer, the Centurion, snatching and crushing. But in The Refugees he changes, his slow sustained appearance is designed not to alarm, he has come for the Mother. He dances with her an elegant little dance, like a pavane, and he receives her with dignity and carries her off cradled in his arms, with warmth and tenderness, so different from his previous appearances. With the Partisan who has killed because of her sense of duty, he comes like a steamroller, pressing through the space with a slow sense of inevitability. He marks the first beat of the bar very strongly, and conveys the idea that anything in the way of this execution will be crushed, not by the attacking gestures of The Battle but by a sustained "there is no stopping me" energy. He has changed once again to suit the situation. In The Brothel he galumphs around like a lecherous clown clasping the Young Girl to him with a leer, a lustful oaf on a drunken night out.

In The Aftermath he has changed again. At the beginning he's strong, taking control of the Old Soldier's actions. There's a strength but it's not costing him anything. As he crosses the stage for the second time it is as though the whole world is at his back. He manipulates them like puppets, beating out the time with the flag very lightly, but getting an instant and universal response from all, then cuts them down as Death the Reaper. Thus we see that each situation he confronts differently, with a different dynamic quality, and it is this dynamic vitality which helps to keep our interest in Death as a character. So often it is the image of Death as a Thunderer which springs to mind, but on closer examination one sees tremendous diversity in dynamic profile. With the Profiteer he becomes like an avenging angel and returns to his former fighting self.

The character of The Profiteer, by contrast, is drawn very simply. He is an 'end-gainer', solely concerned with his objective. His motivation is single-minded greed, an idea conveyed by the frequent use of terminally accented phrases. His sharp, staccato movements are interspersed with sustained gliding movements, which paint him as a

47

very slimy character. In stark contrast to Death his movements are usually in the lighter area of the dynamic spectrum. He has this in common with the Gentlemen in Black. Only in his final battle with Death do we see any real weight or strength, and even here nothing to compete with the crushing power of Death. But he is also a manipulator. In The Farewells he urges the soldiers toward their doom. As he claps his hands together he appears to be in control, but in fact it is the stronger, beating feet of Death whom all must follow.

In The Brothel, the Profiteer really is in complete control. The Young Girl in this scene provides a good example of the expressive uses of movement with contrasting flow. Her own movements are all controlled by other participants in that scene. She herself is out of control, being manipulated by the Profiteer and the soldiers, literally she's tossed around from one person to another. Her free flowing hair typifies her plight - for the first time in the ballet you see that she's taken off her scarf and as she moves she has no control over her hair.

Throughout the ballet Jooss uses rhythm, dynamics, timing and flow all combined together to produce dance which is innately musical. This musicality does not derive from Cohen's music, but rather springs from Jooss's own understanding of the power and expressiveness of eukinetics. In The Gentlemen in Black the music seems almost to play as though in the background. In Death's dance Jooss creates a terrific rhythmic tension by emphasising a 3/4 time dance movement set against the 4/4 time of the music. He creates this rhythmic tension at other places in the ballet, for example The Refugees' music plods slowly and inevitably onward, while the Mother flows around the stage in a way which seems to be trying to ignore the pulse of the music until at one magic moment her steps and the music come into unison, and we know that what must be must be. In the concluding moments of the Partisan Death steps firmly on the musical downbeat. As the Woman approaches her execution, she has her own faltering rhythmic counterpoint. The soldier's final movement is unaccented until the 'shot' is fired.

Laban, with Jooss and Leeder, codified a set of movement principles that articulated the natural laws of movement concerning the human body's relationship to space and space harmony, these he called Choreutics, and those laws concerned with the dynamics and rhythm of movement he called Eukinetics. From this basis Jooss and Leeder together developed a practical working language for use in the theatre. In *The Green Table* we see that language most clearly articulated. Jooss said *The Green Table* was a study in Choreutics and Eukinetics[3], but when we watch the ballet we are not concerned with the fact that The Battle is based on a series of impacts and impulses, or that The Refugees is built around the subtle changing of tensions and relaxations, that the Gentlemen in Black alternate between movement that is indirect or direct, punctuating that movement with a series of clear rhythmic accents, or that the Young Girl in The Brothel attempts to move in a way which is free flowing but is manipulated by the bound flow of all the other characters. What we see is the plight of human beings - their misery, their despair, their fear, their struggle.

Through a process of communication which is kinaesthetic we perceive directly in our musculature the dynamic and rhythmic variations which are present in the bodies of the dancers before us. What started in the mind of the choreographer as an intention or feeling or emotion manifests itself as a particular tension, or form, or motion in the body of the dancer. As an audience we perceive those changing tensions and rhythms, sensing them with our muscles and responding to that muscular sensation with our feeling or emotion (and all this without uttering a word).

Notes

1 Tobi Tobias, Interview with Kurt Jooss for the Oral History Project, The Dance Collection, New York Public Library. September 1976.

2 Ruth Foster, Interview with Kurt Jooss, the Jooss Archiv, Amsterdam. April 1973.

3 Michael Huxley, 'The Green Table - a Dance of Death' *Ballett International* (vol 5, 8/9, 1982), p. 9.

Wright on Jooss

The Director of The Birmingham Royal Ballet, reflects on the work and influence of Kurt Jooss

Peter Wright

My career began with Jooss way back in 1944 when I became an apprentice student with the company he had formed in Cambridge, and World War ll was still raging. Looking back over the last forty-eight years of my work in dance, I am constantly aware of the extra-ordinary influence Kurt Jooss had on me, both as an artist and as a human being. My first meeting with him was at the Arts Theatre Club in London. I was about to leave boarding school determined to become a dancer, and my piano teacher, having previously been a rehearsal pianist with the Jooss Company and School when they were based at Dartington Hall in Devon, had advised me that as I was already seventeen and a bit on the old side to start classical training, this type of dance might be the best solution. He had told me much about Jooss's approach to dance and described many of his ballets, and an opportunity was arranged for me to meet him.

What a difference from the interview that I had had with Ninette de Valois a few days before - she had kept my father and me waiting for two hours at the New Theatre (now named the Albery), given us ten minutes of her time, and been devastatingly honest about my prospects, but at the same time she offered me a place at the Sadler's Wells School. Mr. Jooss, on the other hand, spent a good hour with me, discussed my paintings that he had asked me to bring along, con-vinced me that he and his colleague, Sigurd Leeder, could provide me with the best possible training and painted a wonderfully exciting picture of life in the Ballets Jooss Company. Mind you, he was des-perate for male dancers and de Valois was relatively flush! But they were in very different situations - she was in the process of building up a huge national organisation and, as well as getting the best stan-dard for the present, was planning constantly for the future. Jooss at that time was concentrating solely on keeping a small company together and the performance of his own works. For her, time was of the essence, but for him time never seemed to matter much.

Jooss was the first real artist I had met - he at once struck me as being kind and friendly, and immediately put me at my ease. He then asked me to go to Cambridge where his company was rehearsing, and dance for him. Not knowing the difference between a plié and an impulse and never having been in a dance class in my life, I was very nervous but I used to enjoy hurling myself around in a very uninhibited way; I put a lot of feeling into it and somehow managed to improvise fairly expressively - I actually felt I had impressed him. Apparently he was impressed and at once set about convincing my parents, who hated the thought of their son becoming a dancer, that I had exceptional talent and that if they allowed me to take up this offer of training he would guarantee to make sure that I was properly looked after on tour, working the follow spot, as call boy and generally helping out. You name it - I did it! In return I would get my classes and £1. 10 shillings a week to live on (this had to include paying for my digs and food as well). Although I had never seen the company in performance, I knew this was for me and de Valois and the Sadler's Wells Ballet were temporarily forgotten.

Well I can tell you it was all quite a shock - straight out of boarding school and onto the road, and in wartime! Rationing, drunken landladies, no heating, bombs dropping and unheated trains that always seemed to leave Crewe - most of every Sunday seemed to be spent on Crewe Station, freezing to death, waiting for cancelled connections. But what a beginning it was! This way of working was a huge help to me in the actual learning process. As I was doing it firstly because I desperately wanted to and not because I had been sent to ballet school by my parents, and secondly, because I was actually paying for it myself, I really worked hard. I concentrated and listened, and got the maximum out of every training session and learned about all the different departments - including lighting, stage management, wardrobe - and about all the backstage dos and don'ts which are so important.

51

What wonderful artists I was surrounded by - Jooss himself of course, Sigurd Leeder, who I thought secretly was a bit of a sadist but was a very good teacher and who was still dancing roles such as the Old Soldier in *The Green Table*, the Captain in his own ballet *Sailor's Fancy*, the all-powerful business man in *Pandora* and a rather revolting character in *A Spring Tale* called the Bogey Man! But the greatest influence on my dancing at that time was Hans Züllig, one of the greatest dancers of all time, who was not only a great performing artist but who also knew how to communicate his control and understanding of movement and expression to others - light and shade, tension and relaxation, and the vital part that breathing plays in the dynamics of dance. He was a great master, who also realised the value of classical technique, but above all was such a wonderful example as a performing artist. He really was the best of the best.

Then there was Noelle de Mosa, lighter on her feet than any ballerina I have known since; Ulla Söderbaum, with her wicked sense of humour both on and off the stage, with an unparalleled flow of movement; Rolf Alexander with his amazing breadth of movement and natural facility - he moved like a tiger; Maria Fedro, the striking Polish countess who played all the mother roles which she shared with Maya Rovida, a beautiful and wonderfully expressive dancer, and countless others. All these Jooss trained artists were wonderful examples and influences on my early days.

When I think back, perhaps the strongest influence that Jooss had on me as a dancer was his insistence that all movement and technique must be regarded as means to a beginning, to be used in order to express and communicate ideas, feelings, stories and emotions. Technique for technique's sake was of no interest to him whatsoever. I remember once so clearly when we were asked to create a short choreographic study - we could do exactly what we liked, but no music. Try as I might I could not think of any particular idea, as, for me, everything had to come from the music, but I managed to string together various movements that I had been learning in what I considered to be rather a pleasing way. When I showed it to Jooss he was really quite cross, accused me of wasting his time and that my dance was like a sentence of words that had no meaning. I was, of course, very upset and tried to argue that I considered there was a place for pure dance with no meaning, but, as I had hardly seen any dance other than one performance by a classical company, The International Ballet, my dance awareness was confined to watching classes and rehearsals of the Jooss company, so I hadn't much knowledge to argue my case! At that time there were three other student /apprentices who were considerably older than me - age never really bothered Jooss in those days when he was eager to find artists who could inter- pret his ideas and had no school to draw on. Anyway, although their pieces did express something, Jooss had to admit mine was far better constructed!

It was this sort of influence that was invaluable to me as a dancer, choreographer and producer. Also the inclusion of improvisation in the training - something that I believe to be sadly lacking now in our own training in the classical ballet - was most important. It does so much good, first of all in the development of personality and in mak- ing dancers feel that they are more than just instruments to be used. Secondly, I think it helps with the interpretation of roles and in mak- ing choreography of your own. It also helps you go halfway when working with a choreographer, not just standing there waiting to be told what to do, but actually being involved in a creative way and encouraging the choreographer to go further with a particular train of thought and movement. Not all choreographers welcome this, but a lot do appreciate contributions from their dancers - Jooss certainly did. Improvisation also increases your imagination.

I have no time for the producer who becomes completely bogged down by trying to reproduce a dance in the exact way that the original dancer created it and ignoring the qualities and personality of the artist - imagine if actors, musicians and singers all performed the classical repertoire exactly in the same way! This is one thing that Pa (as we affectionately called Jooss - but not to his face, of course) drilled in to us - respect the choreography at all times but if you are performing and interpreting a solo role it is vital that you find your own way and never get bogged down by technique and theories which can stop the movements and expression having a clear and direct communication with the public. He also wasn't against changing the choreography for an artist if he felt it would improve their performance. He once did that for me in his ballet *Columbinade* when I had returned to the company at the Folkwangschule in Essen in the early 1950s. The role was a sort of Dandy and I had come back to the company greatly improved having worked with Vera Volkova, the great Russian teacher, and been a member of the Sadler's Wells Theatre Ballet for a few years. At that time, although he had always considered that there was some value in the classical training, he was just beginning to realise that Classical Ballet had a great deal to offer. He actually said to me that he wished he had known about real classical training as opposed to the rubbish that was being perpetrated and taught in the German State Opera Houses at that time in the 1920s and '30s, against which (rightly) he rebelled, and he said he would have used it more. In this particular solo from *Columbinade* I had found some of the linking steps awkward and undefined so, together with his wife Aino and a few tactful suggestions from me, he rearranged parts of that solo, even incorporating a few pirouettes and beats (unheard of in his Company in those days), but achieving the same end result. It helped me gain confidence by feeling that I had contributed something and it had also helped me find my own way of performing this role.

I also remember so well when I danced the Standard Bearer in *The Green Table*. In The Aftermath, as the Standard Bearer, when Death finally overpowers him, you are facing the audience down stage and feel Death's command from behind, rather as if drawn by a magnet. Jooss insisted that that moment must be very personal and that it didn't matter if either the actual arm movements were different at every performance or different from other interpreters, provided that you felt the power and strength being drawn out of you. I thought it was wonderful how he gave his artists a certain freedom and how he cleared your mind of all unnecessary thoughts and, in fact, made the thought process that lay behind the combination of movements wonderfully free, so the basic meaning of what you were portraying came across with a clear and direct voice. Mind you, Jooss was on you like a ton of bricks if you over did it especially with facial expression, though he attached great importance to this. Initially he seemed most concerned with focus, eye contact and the gaze always relating to the direction of movement. He hated exaggerated and hammy expressions but even more, he hated blank, vacant faces. He always wanted the facial expressions to be part and parcel of the movement and always demanded that his artists made sure that their faces reflected and mirrored that particular emotion that the piece was about, be it anger, love, joy, desire, terror, pity, or the feeling say, of soaring on the clouds, loving the earth, meanness, power, despair, elation, satisfaction or frustration - all these feelings or emotion were contained in his work.

Jooss himself had a very expressive face and in those early days just after the war, he was out of necessity, through lack of male dancers, performing a great deal - even though he was in his midforties and suffering from a leg injury. I remember vividly the compassionate expression - so moving - when he portrayed the Father greeting the Son on his return in his own version of *Prodigal Son*; and his sexy leer as the King in *Ballade* as he made advances to the young girl, changing to sickening frustration and resignation as he must watch her die through the scheming of his jealous wife. Never, too, will I forget the extraordinary intensity in the expression of horror slashed across the face of the courtier played by Hans Züllig, as he is forced by the Queen to present a poisoned bouquet to the young girl to whom he is betrothed. Amazing too how Jooss's expression could penetrate the stylised make-up used in Death, ranging from frightening power as he trampled all beneath him in the battlefield to the gentleness and compassion he radiated as he took the Old Mother in his arms.

Jooss was very demanding and insisted on rehearsing everything himself, always paying great attention to detail. But he was incredibly slow and, I am afraid, pretty disorganised in those days. He invariably arrived half an hour late at rehearsals mainly because he had been so busy in meetings and then would immerse himself completely in the work in progress. God how we suffered! - freezing rehearsal rooms (fuel was severely rationed in those days) and no canteen to get a coffee (in fact coffee was such a luxury then you couldn't afford it anyway). Jooss was so totally involved in his work that he would be completely unaware that he had kept most of the company hanging around for hours on end without being used. He really would lose all sense of time. It was lucky for him that there were no union rules in those days, otherwise nothing would ever have been finished. At one point we all got so desperate that I, with fear and trepidation, complained about the way he treated us. Surprisingly, he was very understanding and even asked me to help him reorganise his very haphazard rehearsal schedules!

Jooss went to great lengths to help his dancers feel and understand their choreographic relationship, both to space and to other dancers, and certain of his theories have stuck with me forever. As an example, the three space dimensions of up and down, side to side and back and forwards will always for me relate to the difference in quality between these various points, so that up becomes light and airy, down is deep and weighty, sideways across the body is rather introverted and narrow and an open sideways movement becomes generous, wide and extrovert, backwards is withdrawing into oneself, gathering strength in preparation for release forwards, rather like a bow and arrow. What I missed personally, though, were the starting points for most of these exercises, particularly in the diagonal movements - the *shreges* - as in classical dance we always have positions to start at, go through and finish at. Both these aspects are vitally important and I would like to see some of Jooss's theories incorporated in our classical training to help us get more of the dynamics of movement between these various focal points.

One of Jooss's specialities was the art of the waltz - particularly the Viennese Waltz. One of his well known ballets was *A Ball in Old Vienna,* which critics often used to say would be better performed by a classical company and on pointe. Well, I can tell you, they were wrong! Although the ballet was by no means a great favourite of mine, the actual waltz variations and subtleties that these dancers executed

56

were a revelation to me. I have never since seen classical dancers understand the waltz in the way Jooss dancers of that period did. He would spend hours, fascinating hours, making us get the weight just right when you changed direction, so that it became completely natural, and the gentle and subtle use of the feet. Much time was spent discovering where the movement came from, be it the outside hip, the inside leg, the leading foot or the shoulder and so on, and the variations on the waltz steps were incredible. In recent years I have discovered that the best way to see whether someone can really dance or not is to get them waltzing. Giving a series of balancés in different directions can be most revealing! *A Ball in Old Vienna* was always very popular but, I'm afraid, the real core and essence of the ballet was lost on most of its beholders.

My time with Jooss came in two periods. The first of these, from 1944-47, was punctuated by long periods away, as I suffered from a recurring back injury, plus a spell in the army. I was very much the baby of the company in those days (quite an old baby really as Jooss's dancers generally started much later than classical dancers), and not terribly good at working on my own. Jooss did all he could to make sure that I was getting adequate classes and also being quite a philosopher himself, he went to great pains to try and improve my mind - he would often give me extracts from German philosophers like Nietzsche to ponder and think on - but, like all dancers desperate to get on with their training as fast as possible, I was not too responsive, I'm afraid. Gradually, however, I began to realise that the appalling touring conditions were hindering my development and I was not developing a proper technique. So I really had to do something about it. I secretly envied the classical dancers I had met and admired their technique, line and virtuosity, and I realized I needed much firmer discipline than I was getting on tour, where the conditions were so diabolical, as well as doing eight shows a week when I was either appearing in small parts or working the follow spot. Much as I admired Leeder's teaching, I found a lot of it rather unscientific and, for someone with a back injury, really painful and sometimes harmful. So, when the company went off to the States again, I decided not to go, and embarked on serious classical training with Vera Volkova and ultimately joined The Sadler's Wells Theatre Ballet.

My second period was from 1951- 52 when I had decided to leave the Wells and to return to Jooss's Company. I had spent three years with The Sadler's Wells Theatre Ballet and although I had made considerable strides in my classical technique and had benefited enormously from Peggy van Praagh's tuition, I realized more and more that my start had meant unavoidable limitations. I also yearned for Jooss's more dramatic approach to dance. Jooss had formed his company and school again at the Folkwangschule in Essen/Werden and it seemed a good idea to get more experience with his company and consolidate my earlier training. The two worlds were so different and I had considerable difficulty in re-adapting to the very disorganised routine after working in the much more disciplined life in a classical company. However, I had some opportunities and if it weren't for the fact that the company went bust right in the middle of an English tour I think I might well have made my career there. As it was, I had to return to the Wells, cap in hand, and de Valois took me back into the Company. I was really sorry to part company with Poppa Jooss, particularly as I had felt so much more able to dance in his ballets with my classical technique. This was the time when Jooss had seriously started to incorporate classical training in his school and he had very much wanted me to be part of this amalgamation of the two different techniques. But it was not to be.

Many years ago I used to work with The Royal Academy of Dancing production club, which had been founded by Ursula Moreton, then principle of The Royal Ballet School. She had started this to increase dancers' understanding of what went in to creating a ballet production. Very few people in those days knew much about choreography, as a new ballet in the mid-1950s was a rarity. I used to analyse different sections of the choreography of ballets like Act II of *Swan Lake* and *Les Sylphides*, and I also proposed using *The Green Table* as an example of the construction and shape of a work. Unfortunately, this was not considered to be appropriate, as Jooss was not part of the classical scene in this country - a great pity I think, as

Jooss's influence on me as a choreographer and producer of the classics has been enormous and, I believe, there is a huge amount to be learned from analysing the shape and construction of his works - not only *The Green Table, Big City, A Ball in Old Vienna* and *Pavane* which still exist, but also from the other ballets that have now been sadly lost, particularly *Dithyrambus, Weg im Nebel* (The Way in the Fog), *Pandora* and many more that were great examples of floor patterning, of getting the most impact out of an exit or entrance, of balanced groupings on the stage, of brilliant lighting and in how to lead the beholder's eye to the right spot at the right time. *The Green Table* is an excellent example of all these things, but it is one of his early works and his later ballets contained many more superb choreographic ideas, with much to learn from and appreciate. So often I find in new ballets these days, when so much seems to be happening all at once, essential climaxes and details are missed - not only dramatic ones but purely choreographic ones - something that never happened in Jooss's works.

Now I know that great advances have been made in lighting and, of course, we must take advantage of this and move with the times. I do, however, think that Jooss's use and understanding of lighting was masterly. It was, I might say, both very complicated and very simple - complicated in so far as the amount of cues and focusing and constant colour changes were considerable and so exacting regarding musical timing, but very simple in the way he placed his lamps in order to get clear and dramatic effects. On tour he always supervised the lighting rehearsals himself in each different theatre and I learned a lot from this as I had to be present at these sessions, particularly as I would have to work the follow spot during many of the performances. Perhaps one of the most telling effects in *The Green Table* used to be the way each scene ended with a green follow spot on Death, narrowing down to his skull face as the rest of the scene fades into darkness and this face is left staring at the audience with its dreadful warning. However, he apparently later abandoned this effect in favour of a general fade on the whole figure of Death, in my opinion not nearly so telling. Jooss never went in for scenery very much, in fact, apart from

The Seven Heroes, which had simple hangings. Practically every ballet was performed against a black surround and so the lighting was of the utmost importance. This of course helped with the concentration on the dancers, but I think that with the advances made in the understanding of design for dance in recent years, he would have used scenery much more. Part of the reason, of course, was that in the early days there just wasn't any money. In fact, that had been the case all the way through his creative life.

In recent years Jooss and Anthony Tudor became very close friends, and Tudor spent a lot of time in Essen with Jooss - I just wish this friendship had started earlier as I think they found their ideas and aims had so much in common. They would have had the most marvellous influence on each other and, ultimately, on many other people's approach to dance. They were both great thinkers and philosophers and both passionately believed that Dance and Theatre belonged to each other. They both set great store by the use and understanding of musical shape, phrasing, rhythm, dynamics and construction. A pity no-one had the bright idea to do a recorded interview of the two of them in discussion. They, like Balanchine, really understood music and I think this understanding of music is still an area that has not yet really been penetrated sufficiently by the many dance creators of today - crazy really when you think that without it we would be nothing!

One of the last occasions when I saw Kurt (by then he insisted I called him by his Christian name, as he had become more that an artistic leader and guide in my life and was a close friend of our family) was at Covent Garden. We met in the interval after a performance of Ashton's *Enigma Variations*. I thought it had been rather a good performance and I do know the ballet well and cherish many moments in it. I asked him what he thought, expecting him to be as enthusiastic as I was, particularly as he always admired Ashton's work. But no - he agreed there were certain moments of great beauty, but complained about the fussy decor. Also he objected to what he considered to be inappropriate use of virtuosity, such as Wayne Sleep's multiple turns, and couldn't understand why certain lifts were used, particularly when Elgar lifts his wife across his shoulder in her long Edwardian dress. He wanted the whole ballet to be simpler and thought that most of the steps were unnecessary with the exception of Antoinette Sibley's 'Dorabella' solo, which he cited as an example of how classical steps and footwork could be used to great effect to portray a particular character and personality. Although appreciating his point of view, I came away feeling he had missed much of the beauty of the choreography and urged him to see it again. He said he wanted to but sadly never did and anyway, I realised that only rarely does one choreographer like another's work, particularly someone with such very strong ideas about choreography and theatrical communication. Great choreographers seem to have an inner compulsion - they have to do it their way - and nothing will swerve them from their approach to their final goal. A great and extraordinary gift that so few possess. This is what I suppose makes them great, and I certainly count Jooss as one of them.

Kurt Jooss had found and established his own approach to Dance - so valid, so important, and even if *The Green Table* is the only ballet he will be finally remembered for, surely that is enough. What shocks me so is that here is a man who was so active in establishing Laban's Dance Notation and insisted that all his students learned it, but, apart from four ballets, all his other works have been lost and were never recorded. This is tragic when you think how many ballets and operas have failed at first and are later recognised as masterpieces.

I believe Kurt Jooss's influence is very strong and there is a lot we can all learn from his great example - my only fear is that people do tend to become over protective, analytical and theoretical about the great masters of dance who have died, such as Fokine, Tudor, Balanchine and Ashton, to name a few. We do have a great responsibility to ensure that their works really live. The worst thing is for the works they have left us to become museum pieces with no life in them. This has happened so often, particularly with many of the classics, and I believe it to be the responsibility of each generation of producers to make sure that present day audiences can relate to the great works of the past. No mean task! We are indeed lucky to have had people like Anna Markard and Michael Soames to keep the blood flowing in Jooss's and Ashton's ballets.

I am hugely grateful to have worked with Jooss, for his friendship, and for starting off my life in Dance the way he did. One of my most treasured possessions is Noverre's *Letters on Dancing and Ballets*, which he gave me as a Christmas present in 1944, and which bears the inscription 'To Peter, as a good companion on his way'. It is a wonderful book that expresses so well what Jooss himself believed in and has been my Dance Bible ever since. How admirable it is that his work is continuing today and I am so delighted that here in this University, his methods and ideals are being understood and cherished by Clare Lidbury and Andy Adamson, in the very city where my company, The Birmingham Royal Ballet, has made its home. May this vitally important work continue to grow and let us endeavour to learn from each other as much as possible.

Open Forum

A.M. - Anna Markard, H.M. - Hermann Markard
P.W. - Peter Wright, A.A. - Andy Adamson
C.L. - Clare Lidbury, M.P. - Mikaela Polley

The Forum was chaired by Andy Adamson with Anna Markard and Hermann Markard on the panel. Peter Wright and Clare Lidbury were in the audience.

Q   I saw Table *I suppose thirty times before the war and hundreds of times between 1942 and 1947. To me, the point of the scene with the women is that they are going towards their doom without realising it. In your father's time, we never saw Death come on, you never knew he was there until there was a tracker (follow-spot) on his face. Since then I've seen* Table *in Essen, Utrecht and here and I've always been able to see Death come on and sit down. Why is it that with the wonderful lighting technology we have now it's not possible to achieve that situation where you can't see Death?*

H.M.   In the days with Ballets Jooss, the musicians almost played by heart. Now we always get spill from the orchestra pit, on stage. It is very difficult to make the light very dim on the score. It is the piano light that is the problem in every production. The pianists need to be in contact with the stage so have to sit high, not down in the pit. We never get the sort of blackout that we actually want. In addition, yesterday (during the dress rehearsal) there was a blue sheen, possibly because someone forgot to close a door or put out the working lights. These things just happen. The intention is total blackout between scenes.

Q   I too saw The Green Table *in 1942 and 1943, and, memory is fallible, but I remember that the gaps between the scenes were much less. Some of the tension of the ballet disappears if you have a long gap and I don't remember that in performances I saw before.*

H.M.   In the 1960s there were gaps of different lengths - if all the gels needed changing it was a long gap, if only some of the gels it was a short gap. At the end of each scene Death appears and we bring in a different light - a sort of floating light which doesn't touch the stage - and during this the gels are changed. We intended to make all the gaps equal in length.

Q   In sixty years what sort of differences can one tolerate in a ballet that is being reproduced and still say " Yes! It's the same ballet"? Also, in sixty years, has the ballet grown or become a shadow of itself? We don't necessarily expect it to be the same, so what are the differences?

A.M.   *The Green Table* is a very tightly-knit choreographic composition and the composition has remained intact. I think this is probably part of the unique qualities of the work. It has made many points in dance history and I think that it is probably one of the first works to be notated in a comprehensive system of dance notation. Therefore we have the composition, as we have the musical score, and they have then to be directed.

Part of the question probably appertains to the instruments with which we are able to recreate the score and how we direct that. There has been a great deal of change both in the artists with whom we work and in the way audiences expect to receive a performance. This is also my personal situation - we all grow older - and part of this development is something that we all grow with and grow into. So I think we have to say dancers are trained differently, the dancer's instrument has become very versatile. The classical dancer has tremendous technical abilities and we have to work on the "modern" qualities with the classical dancers in order to achieve weight and flow.

Real changes? I've certainly not instigated any at any point, but I think it's very important for those of you who remember the work from the early days, fallible or not, that my father revised, clarified and sifted this work on several occasions during the process of the ballet entering the international repertoire and when there was no longer a Ballets Jooss - the Ballets Jooss having been made up mostly of dancers trained in the Jooss-Leeder system.

Q   Is there anything which you see in a ballet company performing the work which makes you think that there is a difference, perhaps a quality that a modern company couldn't bring to it?

A.M.   I don't have a problem with that because I have worked with companies which have an eclectic repertoire for so many years that I don't even have this division. For me we have versatile dancers who are not so locked into a style. If a company is locked into a style, we simply have to work harder in rehearsal - but we always work hard in rehearsal, no matter with whom. I also have experience of working with quite clearly channelled modern companies. They have their own kind of difficulties to deal with. It is not so that the classically based companies have things to learn that the modern companies do not. We're simply talking about emphases of a different kind in each case, and also a great deal to learn in each case. People don't normally expect modern companies to have a problem with this work.

Q   Who casts it?

A.M.   I work for a short period of time with almost the entire company in little groups working on choreographic material. For a solo role there will be six or eight people working carefully with me and gradually we sift and find out who looks as though they will grow into this role well. It's a very practical process, nothing to do with the status of dancers within the company.

Q   What kind of thing are you looking for? Is it just a versatile technical ability or something else?

A.M. It's certainly not technical facility because one can take that for granted. The qualities that we look for are: musicality; the ability to understand qualities of moving; dramatic talent; sensitivity to understanding style - that sort of thing.

Q   You obviously have two casts here, what control do you have over subsequent revivals and future casting?

A.M. I have very good co-operation with all concerned in the company, so we discuss everything very carefully. We've been working very hard for six weeks with Peter Wright coming to as many rehearsals as he could, with the assistant Artistic Director, Desmond Kelly, working beside me. So we have a very clear understanding about who should grow into things. We have part of a third cast - and there are some very talented people there who haven't had enough rehearsal, but who we would consider. All decisions are made mutually and I would be consulted about future castings.

P.W. It's an understanding that we always consult with our choreographer and those who are restaging someone else's work. It's in our interest as a company to collaborate with the people who put the works on.

Q   How have the dancers responded to the work?

A.M. We had to cross quite a few barriers and it took quite a while, but this is not unusual. *Green Table* is deceptive for the dancers at the beginning of rehearsal time - it appears to be something that you can learn quickly and reproduce. It takes a while for people to grow into it and to understand the subtlety - for instance, to understand that every movement is meaningful and to make those movements, those gestures, really your own, so that you are able to reproduce them with a meaningfulness from the point of view of the dancer, the artist on stage.

Q   How do you achieve that with the dancers? What sort of language do you use to communicate the meaning that you're trying to achieve? Do you describe what it feels like or do you have images that you use?

A.M.   I use everything at my disposal! I demonstrate, I talk, I sing, I scream, I try to be patient. Anything which will help. I'm dependent on the moment, the atmosphere that we have. Seriously, I demonstrate every detail as well as I can so that a lot of the learning process is learning directly from me, learning rhythm, form and content. But beyond that there's so much more that goes into coaching, when you look for any way of helping.

Q   Does that become a major part of the learning process? I presume that the dancers can copy the pictures and the movement, and then does the meaning come with it or after it?

A.M.   It's like learning the words of a play. You are only equipped with the beginning and then you have to make it your own. It is a major part, it's the artistic side of the work, as opposed to work as a repetiteur. I do try to teach form and content simultaneously, but it's very hard to pile everything together.

Q   Do you show the dancers a video?

A.M.   No! They very often want to see a video but I don't think it's necessary. Sometimes it can even get in the way. I believe very strongly that people should find their own way into the role. It's lovely then later to compare, but you have to be secure on a personal interpretation and concept.

Q   We've seen a video of the Joffrey Company and I have the feeling that the performance we saw last night (by The Birmingham Royal Ballet) was much closer to the original. I wonder if you would agree with that?

67

Kurt Jooss: *60 years of The Green Table*

A.M.   The most important thing is that live performance cannot be compared with anything else. But I must defend the Joffrey Company because I've worked with them for a long time very carefully and because they've had a close relationship with *The Green Table*. *The Green Table* has been in their repertoire from 1967 onwards which is quite extraordinary. I think we did four or five brand new *Green Tables*, so there was almost a tradition there. Bob Joffrey used to send the students into rehearsal, saying they had to grow with the work and understand what the values are. I'm glad that our live performance, or rather rehearsal, convinced you more than the video. I do, however, think that the Joffrey video is exceptionally good. We had exceptional conditions in the television studio - they built a stage in the studio and we did a scene a day. Maybe it's too good, too clean.

Q   There is a score and, with the idea of the ballet living on, how much detail is in the score, other than the notation and the music? How are the dynamics, the ideas that actually made the piece, dealt with? If someone else were to reconstruct it from the notation how much information would they receive?

A.M.   I'm not a Labanotation expert and I've been working the other way - by putting information in, not checking what's in there. I'm the wrong person to make that discovery, but there is a lot in there.

Q   You say that you use lots of different ways to get the dancers to do what you want, a special language and some of those things can't be in the score.

C.L.   There are lots of verbal images written alongside the notation in the score.[1] But, I think what you're talking about is the role of the reconstructor, not the notator, in that it is the reconstructor who has the basic score and she who has to make it live for the dancers, choosing the appropriate words or images for the person with whom she is working.

68

A.A.   At the moment Anna fulfils all those roles.

A.M.   I'm very concerned about passing on knowledge, style, everything to do with the question of what should be passed on, so that the work will be understood. I'm sure that it's preserved already.

Q   To what extent do the masks play a role in rehearsal in enhancing the movement?

A.M.   In the case of The Gentlemen in Black I work entirely the other way round. We look at the photograph to set the atmosphere and to see that everyone is wearing a mask at the table. Then we work on the movement and on the meaning of the movement, on the inflections and on the changes in quality, and what those changes of qualities communicate. We wear the masks very late and I have to be very sure with all the dancers that the masks enhance what they do. If they rely on the mask for anything at all, we die! I always say these remarks about not relying on the masks - the scene can die if a percentage of the dancers feel 'it's not me anyway, just the mask' or 'it's only my arms and legs'. It's entirely the reverse - you have to feel who you are, what you are, and what situation you're in. You have to study carefully the choreography and then enhance that and come through the mask. The mask has a personality that you might think swamps what you're doing. If you're successful, your personality will come through the mask. It's a very exciting procedure.

Q   Was the music written before the choreography or was it an ongoing process of creation with the two? Did Jooss provide a detailed synopsis, broken down, or was it a creative process at one and the same time?

A.M.   It was a creative process in the studio and they would have discussion. It was mainly choreography leading as I understand it, but there was a marvellous partnership between the two and mutual respect - so that the musician could come the next day and say

"Listen, I can't deal with this. Can we do this or that so that I can make the phrase?" - this kind of thing. The music was tailored to fit the choreography to a certain extent but only to a certain extent because there really are different voices going on. Sometimes the music is not more than a tapestry on which the instrumentation of choreography takes place. So we are never literally dancing to the music. The music is an integral and complementary element, of course.

P.W.   Have you ever had the experience of someone setting a section of the ballet from notation and then that you've gone and developed it? Or have you always been there right from the beginning? We often have someone ahead to put it on and sort things out and then send the choreographer or whoever along at the end to finalise it.

A.M.   I've only worked that way in an educational situation with college students in America, never with the aim of putting on a production but for testing the score. I've never risked doing what you do because I don't think we're ready to be economical on time. It would be more time consuming that way on company time. I'm looking forward to the time when the score will be up to doing as Peter suggests.

Q   Do you regret that so few Jooss ballets have survived?

A.M.   Of course I regret this greatly, but I have learned to accept it a long time ago. My father has been quoted as saying "at least we have the four", so I tell myself this too. We have a full programme. They are very different works which are unique and we are very fortunate. It's most unfortunate that so much of the work is lost, things like *Journey in the Fog, Company at the Manor,* the humorous as well as the dramatic. It's just the way it is.

P.W.   I think it's a tragedy! It's so sad that only four works are recorded in Labanotation when he supported notation so much. He made all his students learn it. *Song of Youth* was wonderful!

Q   We have examples of works being restaged from the memories of dancers, from photographs, whatever we can dig out. Have you ever considered the idea of doing such a thing with any of your father's 'lost' works?

A.M.   No, I don't think I would. I have a lot of material but I don't think there's any way that one can guess at what the choreography was. I'd be very happy to have young choreographers maybe follow a Jooss libretto, or a musical score, but making their own work from this. I would not at any time consider remembering a phrase and surmising on another.

P.W.   I think it would be worth having a try! We recently, very successfully, revived *Choreartium* - a major work - with no notation. This was done through the memory of dancers and accounts and although obviously not totally accurate, it was well worth doing. There are a lot of Jooss dancers - Hans Züllig and Noelle de Mosa for example - to draw upon and it would be very interesting to see if one could revive something. Four ballets from Jooss's output is actually pretty small!

A.M.   And one only six minutes! I would always help but I would never do it. One would need to say "After Jooss". If someone wanted to try I would agree to that, but I'm not going to do it myself.

P.W.   Obviously *Choreartium* is not one hundred per cent accurate, but it has still maintained the essence of the ballet and brought it to life. I think there are a lot of Jooss's works which are still important like *The Mirror* and *Pandora*.

The discussion with Anna and Hermann Markard came to an end at this point. The forum continued later with Mikaela Polley (the Young Girl from The Birmingham Royal Ballet Company's production of *The Green Table*) joining the panel. Peter Wright was no longer present.

Q   What did you and other members of the Company know of The Green Table before it was announced?

M.P.   *The Green Table* was completely new to me. Peter announced it at the end of last season and gave us a briefing on what it was about. He was in the production himself so he was very knowledgeable about it. As I didn't know very much about it, it was a question of learning it from Anna when she came to teach us.

Q   What were your reactions to what you were presented with?

M.P.   I was very interested in the piece and I'd seen the video so I had an idea of what to expect. Anna was very helpful - before we learned anything she went over what the part you were doing entailed, what you had to bring across.

Q   So you got the interpretation before the movement?

M.P.   Yes.

Q   How strange was the movement?

M.P.   It was quite strange because it wasn't the usual classical technique which we're used to, it's a different kind of movement all together. It was quite strange to begin with, but bit by bit it became easier.

Q   What were the strangest things?

M.P.   The use of the body - in classical technique you're very upright. In *The Green Table* there's a lot of curling and use of the back, so that was a different way of using the body entirely.

Q   How did you set about overcoming that difficulty, that new experience?

M.P.   It was really a question of just practising, looking at your body in the mirror to begin with to see the position you have to make, and then going away and feeling the position yourself. So it was programmed in my head, how to feel the movement.

Q   Have you had any modern or contemporary training?

M.P.   I did stage modern and tap when I was younger. I went to the Royal Ballet School when I was sixteen and they had contemporary classes on a Saturday.

Q   Is what you did in those classes similar to what Anna's been doing with you?

M.P.   It's similar to the contemporary training I had, which wasn't very much, in the use of the body - curling and contracting the body - so in a way it did help in that it wasn't completely new.

Q   You mentioned being in front of the mirror and seeing the shape and getting the feeling. Can you explain a little more about how that works for you.

M.P.   All our studios are built with mirrors so its very easy to make a shape and see yourself in the mirror. But as soon as you turn away from it you can't feel your arm in its proper position if you're constantly looking in the mirror. It's important to feel the shape away from the mirror before you get on stage because on stage you can't see yourself. You have to know exactly what your body's doing.

Q   What about going into the movement - because you can't do that with a mirror can you, you just see the form?

M.P.   You can see the form with the mirror but, when you're doing the movement in its entirety, if you're looking in the mirror your head would be at the wrong position so it wouldn't have the whole flow of the movement.

Q   *You seem to be approaching the movement by getting the shape first. Did that then give you the feeling or did you ever get the feeling and see if that then gave you the movement?*

M.P.   I think it's a mixture of the two - you can approach it from both ways. You can try and do the shape and if it doesn't look right you can go away and think about it and do it from the feeling, and maybe the shape will come naturally.

Q   *Where does the feeling come from?*

M.P.   Inside you.

Q   *If you don't know what it is, how do you get the feeling? What does Anna say to you?*

M.P.   You have to know already what you're trying to portray so, for example, the Young Girl in The Brothel scene is constantly trying to get away from all the soldiers, so the movement is long and reaching, and you've just got to feel the reaching and try to get further and further away. That's how I try to do it.

Q   *Do you always have to understand the feeling that the shape makes or is the shape enough? Do you have to be able to define the feeling?*

M.P.   To a certain extent - you can't show a feeling without feeling something.

Q   *How do you get at feeling experiences which you yourself have not experienced? I mean, I don't suppose you've been in a brothel!*

M.P.   In that case you have to use your imagination, and imagine yourself in that situation.

74

Q   What do you think about when you're dancing in The Brothel?

M.P.   I imagine myself in that situation. I have to dance with three soldiers and I don't actually want to be in the brothel, so I have to imagine that there is this person who's forcing me to dance with them and that's not what I want to do. As such, when I get the chance, I try to escape. I have to try to imagine myself in that situation and how I'd feel. You have to imagine that where the wings are is a wall, and you're trying to get through that wall. That's what I try to think about.

Q   When you do that, do you go through stages when you learn so that when you're first starting off rehearsals you're more concerned with what you've got to do and then afterwards free yourself to think or do you do it the other way round?

M.P.   Yes. I like to know what the steps are so I know exactly what I'm doing, they're in my head, and then it does free you to interpret. Your feet will go where they're supposed to and you can work on other things. That's the way I work.

Q   Have you had any acting experience? I wonder, if you have, could you talk about your work on The Green Table from that point of view?

M.P.   I haven't really had any acting experience. I did a little bit of drama at school and at the Royal Ballet Upper School. They had some mime classes and a small amount of drama. That helped.

A.A.   Actors have a method based on Stanislavsky's approach to the theatre which enables them to go through systematically filling in the details of a character for which they have no experience. They talk about 'emotional recall' trying to make sense of things in their own life that might relate to the situation in which they find themselves. Do dancers ever do this? Would it be useful to dancers?

75

M.P.   It would probably be something that would be useful because you could bring things that have happened to you in a similar situation. I've never been in a brothel but I may have been in a situation where I've desperately wanted to leave, so to use that as an interpretation would be useful.[2]

Q   Can we go back to talking about the way you prepared yourself. When you took class was the class exactly the same or was there any variation? Would you have liked a variation?

M.P.   Class was still the same as we usually have. It might have been nice to have some classes based around the technique to help with it.

Q   Would you have liked to have taught a class, Anna, or were you happy with the dancers taking their normal class?

A.M.   I think many people don't realise what dancers are in for today. Mikaela and her colleagues were racing from one rehearsal to another and this means from one style to another. They are rehearsing simultaneously *Romeo and Juliet, Symphonic Variations, Snow Queen, The Green Table,* and several other things. So we are all of us in an extreme bind. Daily class cannot accommodate any of this - daily class is daily class. It's more a security requirement than anything else just to keep going, not to lose your stamina, your teaching. I would be very happy to be able to teach a little before we ever go into production - I think it would help the dancers enormously. I would feel, because I'm very much a teacher, that I would be able to equip people more thoroughly with the movement material that is in *The Green Table* if we were able to work at it a little systematically as opposed to purely what the dancers need in order to set the choreography. But this is an illusion, it is impossible to find either the time or energy on either side. I could ask somebody to teach for me, but the company wouldn't have time. It's just not possible, very unfortunately.

Sometimes I get into an educational situation and then it is possible, and these situations can be very positive.

M.P. I would agree with that. Some people are involved in five things and are rushing from style to style. We just don't have the time.

Q   Is this a problem that you encounter all the time, regardless of the shift of style from ballet to ballet, that nobody has the time to teach you their own personal language or the language of a particular ballet, they just teach you the movement?

M.P. Yes it's the problem that we always have especially at the beginning of the season when we've got so many new productions going on.

Q   Have you found that the way you've been working on The Green Table *has affected the way you've been working on the other ballets or do you completely cut off when you go into other rehearsals?*

M.P. I don't cut off completely, but I see it as a special piece in which that technique is special for that piece. But it's dramatic qualities can help you because you don't always get the chance to do dramatic pieces, so it can help for later on. You can think 'how did I go about tackling that role' and it can help you in that way.

Q   When you're in a classical ballet do you work on the expression or is it purely technique?

M.P. Some pieces of classical ballet you can rely purely on technique, but I see a classical dance in terms of feeling and expression, not just the technique. You can't get by on just that! I think it comes from inside - that's what makes very special dancers.

Q   I presume in a classical ballet the amount of emotion you can feel is somewhat restricted because there are only certain forms and

77

certain techniques you can apply. Have you found in The Green Table, *where the movements are derived from emotion to start with, that you can feel these emotions more fully?*

M.P. Yes. Anna's very clear in saying it - if you're reaching towards someone, that you're actually trying to reach them. You've not just got your arm there looking like you're reaching, you are actually trying to. That completes the whole movement.

Q Do you feel restricted when you go back to classical ballet?

M.P. In some ways, not all ways. Even though you have the set classical technique, you're not just putting your arms in positions. You have to feel the positions in your body and that can create quite a different effect from just putting your arms there.

Q The dramatic, expressive qualities that dancers are called on to demonstrate in all kinds of different ballets do not seem to be adequately covered in your training. It seems that some dancers have it and some dancers haven't. It's a kind of gift and nobody seems to give you the ground work, training or exercises in order to get better at this or prepare you properly.

M.P. That's very true. You can be thrown in to something which needs you to call on this dramatic training and sometimes it's left to you to find it yourself. There's not enough training or advice given.

Q So this means that you, Anna, in putting on the ballet were given a number of dancers and you chose Mikaela because you felt that she had these dramatic, expressive qualities, which presumably some of the other dancers whom you could have chosen didn't have. Would that be fair?

A.M. In a sense, yes. But of course there are many other aspects as well. As I mentioned earlier we do always work in larger groups and

for many reasons these larger groups become smaller and smaller until we find that we have to make decisions for practical reasons. We are restricted in time so we have to make decisions and then we have three people working on each role and that's it. I have the difficult task of making these decisions.

Q   Anna provides a very challenging environment which may draw out the best, but on the other hand it's a sort of competition isn't it?

M.P.   It is slightly at the beginning when five names go up for one role and you're all fighting for it. It gives you a competitiveness.

Q   And is it really competitive?

M.P.   It's healthy competition not nasty! You're doing it for yourself, not because you don't want someone else to do it.

Q   What relationship do you have with the second cast Young Girl?

M.P.   It's been a very close relationship because we've worked together, watching and learning from one another. You can see things that maybe she can't see and maybe vice versa. We like to give each other help.

Q   Did Peter Wright talk to you about the qualities you're show-ing in the ballet?

M.P.   Not really. He spoke a bit about the piece before he told us we were doing the production. Then when Anna came over to teach us all casting was left with her, as we worked with her.

Q   What about the music? Do you react to the music of this ballet any differently from your reaction to the music of other ballets?

M.P.   In all cases I feel that the music is a very important part. You can't just separate it from the dance, that this is the dance and that music is going with it. You have to listen to the music, it has to come in to your body and then you interpret the music as well.

Q   In Symphonic Variations *the dance is almost a visualisation of the music but in* The Green Table *as a dancer you've got your own melody line. Is this any harder to do, or easier to do because you don't have to go with the music?*

M.P.   It is with the music. It is probably easier for me to understand it because I've heard the music time after time and for me the steps do go with the music. Maybe you're not hearing the same thing that I'm hearing underneath?

Q   So you're locked on to certain things in the music?

M.P.   Yes.

Q   Could I ask you about partnering? Obviously the partnering is going to be a little different from partnering in a classical ballet?

M.P.   There is no partnering like in classical technique as in partnered pirouettes or promenades. It's very much a bonding of the two dancers. It's more of a bonding than 'put your hand there' or 'turn her from there'. It's feeling each other and working it from there, working as a couple, almost as one, moving through the movements.

Q   Is that a new approach to you?

M.P.   It is a new approach and it's very helpful because it's important in classical dance when you're partnering someone you're not two separate bodies doing the movement. You've got to work with each other. That's very important.

Notes

[1] The score referred to here is that being prepared by Odette Blum of the Dance Department at The University of Ohio, from the notation of Gretchen Schumacher, undertaken as part of a Dance Notation Bureau Project, begun in 1980.

[2] Leo Kersley added: " This company in its early days used to have Stanislavsky classes. They went on for about three years but they ended up in riots simply because half of us realised that there is a way of performing by doing it from the inside and part experience. But the very best performer in the company - perhaps the best they've ever had - didn't work that way at all. That was Robert Helpmann and he did it purely on technique."

Appendix 1

Conference delegates attended one of the dress rehearsals of the opening programme of The Birmingham Royal Ballet's Autumn Season on Saturday 18th October, 1992. The evening began with David Bintley's *Flowers of the Forest* (music by Malcolm Arnold and Benjamin Britten, designed by Jan Blake, and lighting by John B. Read). This was followed by Frederick Ashton's *Symphonic Variations* (music by César Franck, designed by Sophie Fedorovitch, lighting by John B. Read, and produced by Michael Somes, assisted by Judy Maelor Thomas). The final item in the programme was Kurt Jooss's *The Green Table*.

The Green Table
a dance of Death in eight scenes

Book and choreography	Kurt Jooss
Music	F.A. Cohen,
Design	Hein Heckroth
Lighting and masks	Hermann Markard,
Staging	Anna Markard Jooss, assisted by Gerald Binke.

Death	Kevin O'Hare
Standard Bearer	Peter Ottevangar
The Young Soldier	Paul Bayes-Kitcher
The Young Girl	Anne Little
The Woman	Dorcas Walters

The Old Soldier	Toby Norman Wright
The Mother	Sherilyn Kennedy
The Profiteer	Vincent Redmon
Soldiers	Andrew Allen, Lee Fisher, David Dawson
Women	Louise Britain, Michela Centin, Deborah Noakes, Jane Sparks, Monica Zamorova
Solo Pianos:	Jonathan Higgins, Ross Williams